Are you pessimistic about the future of th [   ] you. Not that Steve McAlpine is unrealisti [   ] But he gives us reasons for hope and ideas for action. Eschewing superficial or trendy solutions, *Futureproof* digs deep into Scripture to prepare us to live well in our changing context and offer true hope in an anxious world.

Tim Chester, Faculty Member, Crosslands Training

If, like me, Stephen McAlpine's previous book caused you to ask, "Where do we go from here?", here is the answer. It has the same clarity and punchy impact as before. A really good and profoundly helpful book.

Alistair Begg, Senior Pastor, Parkside Church, Cleveland, Ohio

A positive, encouraging read for anyone wondering whether Christianity has a hope of surviving the decades to come. (Spoiler: it does, and has a great hope to offer the culture, too.)

Jennie Pollock, Author, *If Only*

It's often said that it's far easier to expose the failings of our society (and the church) than it is to suggest healthy, realistic and, above all, manageable responses—but Steve has managed to do both beautifully. As well as continuing to reflect on the bewildering changes going on in our world, this book offers a richly biblical, sane and thoughtful way forward. Read this book, be encouraged and throw yourself into God's great project to offer hope to a hopeless world!

Gary Millar, Principal, Queensland Theological College

I invariably find Stephen McAlpine a trusted and insightful commentator on current events, and especially on the relationship between the church and the culture around it. In *Futureproof* he sets his sights on *future* events and offers commentary that is just as helpful and just as perceptive— commentary that will help the church live well in this day and prepare itself for days soon to come.

Tim Challies, Blogger; Author

This is so helpful for all sorts of Christians to read. Steve manages to combine nuanced gracious engagement with Western values, alongside specific practical suggestions. He offers shrewd cultural comments and observations but they are always driven by biblical priorities.

Matt Fuller, Senior Minister, Christchurch Mayfair, London

How to live for Jesus in a culture that keeps on changing

Stephen McAlpine

Futureproof

Futureproof
© Stephen McAlpine, 2024.

Published by:
The Good Book Company

thegoodbook.com | thegoodbook.co.uk
thegoodbook.com.au | thegoodbook.co.nz | thegoodbook.co.in

Cover design by Faceout Studio | Art direction and design by André Parker

ISBN: 9781784989422 | JOB-007618 | Printed in India

To Jill, Sophie and Declan, for walking into the future with me with gospel grace. And to the staff at Mimz Barber Shop, for the beard-trims, the banter and the curiosity about the matters in this book.

Contents

Introduction

So you're outside church on Sunday after the evening service when the DeLorean sports car from the classic '80s movie *Back to the Future* suddenly appears hissing and steaming in the car park. The famous gull-wing doors creak open. Emerging from the plume of smoke, an older—much older—version of your pastor runs over to where your startled fellow congregants are milling around.

"Quick!" he shouts breathlessly, fumbling around in his pocket. "We don't have a moment to lose! I'm your pastor from 30 years in the future. Things have changed. They've changed a lot. I've drawn up a list of things you're going to have to start working on now if you want our church to be around then."

Once you've gotten over the craziness of what has just happened, you all gather round him, eager to hear what the future will be like. Questions about hoverboards and their actual existence fade away as this future pastor breathlessly maps out the twists and turns of culture and society coming down the line.

You all lean in as he describes the way governments will view their citizens; the scientific advances that will call into question what it means to be human; the culture's vision of the good life; the place and role of Christianity in society, and whether it will have a role or a place that is even recognisable to us today. He unpacks how environmental and social challenges will be being tackled—or not being tackled.

All of this presents direct challenges to the church. All of it calls for a considered decision by the church to put into place a discipleship program that will be an effective counter to the more challenging aspects of the future secular culture. But you're beginning to feel confident that your pastor from the future has given you enough insight for you to know what to do from this point on. He's filled in the picture distinctly enough for you to know where the key challenges lie.

All too soon he looks up. "Time's up! I've got to go now or I'll miss my moment!" Despite protests and pleadings from some in the group who want to hear more, he is insistent. And within no time at all, the DeLorean screeches out of the car park and down the road, a row of sparks lighting up the air behind it. A police siren suddenly wails close by. Clearly someone was doing 88 mph in a 30 mph zone.

A Futureproof Church

Our culture is constantly changing. Wouldn't it be incredibly helpful if someone from the future came back to help your church figure out how to remain faithful and fruitful within those changes? It would clear your mind if someone were able to tell you some tried-and-tested strategies for navigating a Western world that is hostile to the gospel message, a workplace that is devoted to values not aligned with Christian ones, or an online culture that sweeps people up in ways that seem impossible to predict. After all, who knows what is coming down the line and how it will affect Christians? How do we futureproof ourselves?

This book is not a crystal ball. I can't give you a definitive guide to exactly everything that is going to happen. It's all well and good being a futurist, but what we know as "black-swan events"—once-in-a-lifetime things like September 11 or the COVID-19 pandemic—inevitably upset the best- (and worst-) laid plans of mice and men.

Nor is this book a litany of complaints about ways in which the church is failing to keep up with the culture or speak into the culture, or anything else. If I wanted to see such a list, then I'd only have to go on Facebook and read through my feed for 15 minutes. It seems everyone has an opinion on what the problem is and how the church is supposed to fix it—or how the church is part of the problem.

But I do know for a cast-iron fact that the church *is* futureproof. And I want to help us think through why, and how we can lean into that in a way that prepares us for whatever twists and turns our culture takes in the next 30, 50 or 100 years.

The Task Begins Now

Because of the death, resurrection, ascension, rule and imminent return of Jesus, the future of the church is assured. Jesus himself made that claim when he stated that the gates of hell would not stand up to the advance of his church (Matthew 16 v 17-19). If the worst of the worst cannot stop the inevitable triumph of Jesus and his church, then nothing lesser can. Yet of course that does not mean we just sit back and wait. The discipleship task for those who know that the future is assured *then* is to do the work of futureproofing the church *now*. We're working our salvation *out*, if you like—in the knowledge that God is working it *in* (Philippians 2 v 12-13). We need to ensure that we are readying and equipping ourselves now for whatever the future looks like.

This task begins now. We will not get to the future and be able to shore up non-existent foundations. The time to build communities that will be resilient and strong in the face of perhaps hostile governments is now. The time to grow in a gospel hope that renders us non-anxious and open-hearted in a fearful and shrivelled age is now. The time to put aside every weight of individual and collective sin in order to be holy and hopeful in a godless and nihilist era is now.

This book is designed to help us begin the futureproofing process: not by predicting every minute detail of the future (and especially not the existence or otherwise of hoverboards) but by examining the directions and convictions of our society across a wide spectrum of issues, and then extrapolating out from there to see where they might take us. It will explore Western culture's anxieties about the future and how these anxieties play themselves out.

Armed with these broad insights, we will then take what the Bible says and apply it to a variety of possible future pressures, exploring how we can live for Jesus in a constantly changing culture. Not just for our own sakes but for the sake of the anxious who are looking for hope in times of rapid and nausea-inducing change.

This Scripture still stands:

> *His divine power has given us everything we need*
> *for a godly life through our knowledge of him who*
> *called us by his own glory and goodness.*
>
> *(2 Peter 1 v 3)*

Fun fact: *every* generation of God's people has been futureproofed. We have everything we need. Time to figure out how that is going to play out in practice in this changing and challenging age.

1. The Church of Back to the Future

Events catch us out. I began writing this book in my study, with sun streaming through the windows, my newsfeed filled with images celebrating the Platinum Jubilee of Queen Elizabeth II. There were articles recounting the 70-year reign of an iconic monarch; pictures of crowds of people across the United Kingdom holding street parties and draped in Union Flags; and messages of support and admiration from across the world and the political spectrum. President Joe Biden of the USA, President Emmanuel Macron of France, our newly elected prime minister in Australia, Anthony Albanese, and many others lined up to praise the amazing 96-year-old whose rule had spanned a period that began just after the Second World War.

In that first draft I wrote about the joyous celebrations, colourful and unanimous in their affirmation that her reign, just as much as the equally famous reign of

Elizabeth I back in the days of Shakespeare, was something worth celebrating. In the midst of all the tumult—internationally, nationally, and indeed personally within her own family—the queen had literally been regal, a steady hand in unsteady times.

Yet several months later, as I began editing this book, my daughter—who loved the queen—was texting me, worried that the monarch was about to die. It had been a constant concern for her as the queen had become frailer. And in fact, Elizabeth II did pass away that very day.

It turned out that the Platinum Jubilee celebrations were indeed the final hurrah. Not just for the queen, but for the way of life that she embodied, the values she espoused. The queen's reign represented a period of change like no other in recent history, as we moved from the industrial age of World War II through a technological age in the Cold War era and into our current digital age. The Western world is incredibly different to the way it was when Elizabeth was crowned.

But the changes run deeper than that. Think about this: Elizabeth only became queen because her uncle, Edward VIII, abdicated so that he could marry the love of his life, the divorced American socialite, Wallis Simpson. Elizabeth's father—and ultimately Elizabeth herself—only ascended the throne because the marriage of the king of England to a divorced woman was a bridge too far. The Church of England would not countenance it because Simpson's ex-spouse was still living.

Yet now? The new king, Charles, divorced Princess Diana. He married his lover, the equally divorced Camilla Parker Bowles, whose ex-husband still lives. But there were no formal objections to Charles taking the throne—neither from Parliament nor from the Church of England.

Things have changed, and changed a lot. And of course, by the time you are reading this, things will have moved on apace. Change will have been our only constant. And clearly not always change for the better.

The shift in the moral standards that we demand from a king is only one symptom of the huge differences that now shape our world. It's clear, for example, that we are more divided than ever. Every time a new prime minister or president arrives on the scene, they promise to bring unity—and that lasts a couple of weeks before the hostilities recommence. Division is deeply entrenched. Both sides of politics increasingly see the other as not simply wrong but "bad" or "evil". Polls back this up. In the US, an Axios survey discovered that roughly half of Democrats and Republicans view the other side as both ignorant and spiteful, with a mere 2-4% viewing the other as "kind", "fair" or "thoughtful".[1]

Social media amplifies and rewards these divisions. We no longer read as widely as we once did, preferring to consume media that confirms what we already think, rather than pushing into ideas that we find troublesome or challenging to our view of the world. Meanwhile Twitter bots, created and backed by rogue governments, are poisoning our politics. Smartphones and social media have radically changed how we communicate with each other and how we absorb information on everything from what a politician did or didn't say to what kind of nappies we should buy. The looming shadow of AI promises more changes still—with unresolved issues around copyright, privacy and employment just starting to peep over the horizon.

What about what it means to be human? It seems impossible nowadays for government health departments to define what a woman is—something that activists applaud, comedians mock, and corporations enforce. Parents are faced with radical "diversity programs" in their children's schools. What do we do when our children announce that their best friend now has a different gender, or they themselves do?

Meanwhile church attendance in Western countries is collapsing with the rise of the "nones" and the "dones". In Australia in 2022, the proportion of people self-identifying as Christians shrank to 44%, down from 61% just ten years prior.[2] This is repeated across the Western board.

Questions arise. Can our public ethics—grown as they are from biblical roots—be maintained in a post-Christian setting? For believers, what is going to happen as the Christian sexual ethic goes from being viewed as merely wrong to being denounced as bad, dangerous and unsafe? Is it only a matter of time before our governments and courts legislate to remove children from parents deemed "unsafe" for holding to a Christian vision of human identity and flourishing? It seemed unthinkable a decade ago, but not now.

We can predict trends and patterns. We can watch decisions made in one year come to their logical conclusions in the next. But the pace of change and the sharp turns mean many of us are suffering from a cultural nausea. It would take an exceptionally confident person to say with any certainty what the next five years will look like, never mind the next 30. The future is a roller coaster, not a cable car. Strap yourself in!

The Future of King and Church

If you have read all of this without having heart palpitations, then check your pulse! Much of what I have described is very confronting—to Christians and secularists alike. It's no surprise that the level of anxiety in the West has skyrocketed. My wife is a clinical psychologist, and she is booked out for months. During the delayed Tokyo Olympics in 2021, she made the point that if there were a mental-health Olympics, anxiety would be the absolute gold-medal winner. Anxiety lies over our Western culture like a pall.

Yet, as Christians, who are called not to be anxious both by Jesus and the New Testament writers, we have a sure foundation for the future, grounded in the resurrection and return of King Jesus. Our King is one day coming to rescue his subjects, and he will usher in a new creation. This should make it possible for Christians to banish that crippling society-wide anxiety, replacing it with hope and confidence.

In fact, it was in the midst of their own turmoils in a brutal Roman Empire that the earliest Christians found their hope for the future. To their joy and surprise, they realised that the future had already begun in the resurrection of Jesus:

> Blessed be the God and Father of our Lord Jesus Christ! In his great mercy, he has given us a new birth into a living hope through the resurrection of Jesus Christ from the dead, and into an inheritance that can never perish, spoil or fade. This inheritance is kept in heaven for you. (1 Peter 1 v 3-4)

Those words were written by the apostle Peter—a man who at one time was so anxious about his own personal future that he even lied about knowing Jesus (Matthew 26 v 69-75). What had changed? The resurrection had convinced Peter that Jesus was indeed God's King, and that if he could conquer death, there was nothing outside his power. This enabled Peter, from that point on, to live large! To live anxiety-free.

Now of course there is a type of anxiety that is part and parcel of every human life—perhaps about matters such as the health or fate of a loved one. The apostle Paul admitted to feeling anxiety in his concern for the church (2 Corinthians 11 v 28). But Paul's anxiety was not the crippling, pervasive anxiety we see in our culture today. Australian pastor and author Mark Sayers sums this difference up:

> In our day anxiety has become one of the significant ailments of our world. Yet it is also a signal that something is desperately wrong in our world. We must differentiate between the individual mental health challenge of anxiety, which a minority of individuals in every culture experience, and the systemic anxiety that our contemporary culture's structures create.[3]

Only a non-anxious structure can counter an anxious one. And the church can be a non-anxious structure, no matter what the circumstances of the future hold. It ought to be, given our understanding of Jesus and his kingship. As Paul wrote:

> The Lord is near. Do not be anxious about anything, but in every situation, by prayer and petition, with thanksgiving, present your requests to God. And the peace of God, which transcends all understanding, will guard your hearts and your minds in Christ Jesus. (Philippians 4 v 5-7)

The Lord Jesus is not merely nearby in terms of proximity; he is nearby in terms of his return! The King is coming. We can pray to God and be guarded by his peace.

Paul's words are not so different to the comfort that Jesus offered in Matthew 6:

> *Therefore I tell you, do not worry about your life,*
> *what you will eat or drink; or about your body,*
> *what you will wear ... The pagans run after all*
> *these things, and your heavenly Father knows that*
> *you need them. But seek first his kingdom and his*
> *righteousness, and all these things will be given to*
> *you as well. (v 25, 32-33)*

Anxiety about the future can be banished by the fact that God is our heavenly Father. God sits in heaven—and the key point here is not his distance from us but his rule over us. His is the kingdom. God has control of all things, even our futures. We don't need to worry.

This lack of anxiety—or at least the conditions that can banish anxiety—must be Christianity's best-kept secret! I am not sure that, if the general public were asked to provide some of the defining characteristics of the church, the term "non-anxious" would be top of the list. But it ought to be.

Being a Christian does not preclude worry or fear. We ought to take seriously the anxiety experienced by those with mental-health issues within our church communities. Yet as an entity, we should not be defined by anxiety. Neither fear about the future nor anger about the increasingly post-Christian direction our Western culture is heading in should be features of a church confidently awaiting the day of Jesus' return.

So, yes, unlike the world, which does not know God or the power of his resurrected Son, we can be confident in our eternal future. But what about in between now and then? What if this book is written, edited, published, distributed and sold, and you still find yourself reading it in a state of anxiety about the future? What about this "now/not yet" interim period before Jesus' return? How do we deal with the increasingly confronting and complex issues that the church is facing?

The Anxieties That Christians Face Now

If Christian blogs, podcasts and political movements are good indicators, then all the signs tell us that in this present age many Christians *are* anxious about many things. There is certainly a sense that we are "abiding a long defeat", whether that's around ethical matters, church attendance figures or influence in the public square.

One of the major things we are anxious about is the manner in which the self-fulfilment mantra of our age is at odds with—even at loggerheads with—the Christian understanding of what it means to flourish as a human. We might call this "the meaning-and-purpose question". Our secular society promises us that we can find ultimate meaning and purpose as we look within ourselves. Self-discovery—finding our authentic self— can provide every resource needed to achieve fulfilment and happiness. Anything that restrains self-fulfilment is a threat to individual and social wellbeing. This stands in stark contrast to the words of Jesus, who declared that anyone who wanted to be his disciple and see life in the age to come must deny themselves and take up their cross (Luke 9 v 23). Mind you, it doesn't take much of an online search to discover that some churches have swallowed the cultural Kool-Aid.

This self-fulfilment mantra is not only looking for converts but is presenting itself in the most attractive way possible. I work in Sydney on a frequent basis, and a drive or walk down that city's Oxford Street during Pride Month demonstrates that the self-fulfilment story is colourful, popular and interested in signing up new members. And with statistics showing that young Christians fall away from the faith at an alarming rate when they go to university, there is a very real concern that we are losing a generation of young people to a program of self-fulfilment that rejects the idea of self-denial altogether, especially in terms of sexuality and identity formation.

Another thing we are anxious about is the fracturing nature of our society: the loss of true community. As Christians we feel this deeply. Indeed, in the past three decades there has been an explosive growth in books about church and what it means to be it and to do it—a sign that our communities are under pressure. Church attendance for those who still claim to be Christian is far more sporadic than in the past. Regular attendance might now be considered one in three Sundays. How can we sustain relationships with people we barely know? How do we do church discipline or church pastoral care when relationships are so thin? And volunteerism has dropped off at an alarming rate.

Meanwhile, our society offers us the promise of deeper connection with ourselves and deeper unity with others, both through advances in science, social sciences and technologies and through a rejection of past traditions. The immersive technology of the metaverse and the manner in which social media is supplanting face-to-face relationships means that even supposedly regular churchgoers are increasingly looking to online experiences. It's an attitude that is alien to the old idea of life-on-life relationships, grounded in a theology that says the local church is a body containing many members. This sense of communal fracturing was fast-tracked by the pandemic; the return to church that many leaders anticipated does not seem to have materialised.

Another anxiety for Christians is that the church may not simply become sidelined in our Western setting but may actually cease to function or exist in any recognisable or meaningful way. Never mind "Does the church have a future?"—the real question, for many, is "Does the future have a church?" Statistics are not our friends here. While some countries such as the USA are coming off a high base of church attendance and therefore have some fat and cultural cachet to play with, the level of religious commitment in the UK has dropped so dramatically that it is possible to imagine a time when Christianity will be a thing of the past there. In my home country of Australia, too, the nominal Christian is giving way to the post-Christian.

This has led to all sorts of calls to reduce funding for Christian institutions and to direct efforts towards other communities. Because the census data is showing less religious adherence, people are starting to ask why governments are funding faith-based schools that have discriminatory staffing practices (only hiring Christians). Or why aged-care facilities that cater to religious communities are being subsidised, in a way that discriminates against ageing same-sex couples. Should they be funded at all if they won't align with societal values?

There is a growing confidence among secular progressives that the church is being increasingly rejected, its voice more and more silenced, and its influence waning— to the point that soon it will no longer be taken into consideration when public policy is being formed. And for many, that is something to celebrate. The church has for too long abused its privilege, and now those days are over.

Wherever we turn—whether we're looking at politics, sexual ethics, religion, education, or any other area of life—we seem to confront fears and threats. It's hard not to wonder what the future holds and what will become of the church. When we read Jesus' question, "When the Son of Man comes, will he find faith on the earth?" (Luke 18 v 8), the best response might seem to be a mumbled "I hope so, but the evidence isn't strong!"

What Must Be Done in the Present?

Given all of this hostility and upheaval, you might be forgiven for thinking that the best approach is for us all to buckle up, quietly fold our wings, and settle into a privatised and personal piety that is a baptised version of our individualistic age. To sit back and wait for the return of the King. To let the present take care of itself and wait it out in a religious bunker.

I hope you can see that the Bible would not permit us to do that. Indeed, the return of the King might find us out if we do! The parable of the talents in Matthew 25 takes a dim view of the inactivity of those to whom the gifts of God have been given. There is a churlish mean-spiritedness to the wicked servant who buries what his master has entrusted to him.

But quite apart from the warning in the parable, there is every reason to be confident that the King who entrusts us with his riches is more than capable of ensuring that we acquit ourselves well with their use. Yes, I believe that the church in the West is going to face significant challenges: there will be increasing pressure on the people of God as we seek to faithfully engage our broken and fallen world with the gospel. But I also believe that there are Spirit-empowered strategies we can put in place *now* in order to be a faithful and flourishing people living under the rule of King Jesus *then*.

There is no guarantee that Jesus will return in our desired timeframe. Yet we have no reason to be anxious, because even if the timeframe is not guaranteed, the outcome is! We don't have to waste energy being anxious; we can put it to better use. We do not want to arrive at some point in the future having squandered an opportunity to prepare for the pressures the church will be facing, simply because we could not get our heads above the cultural anxiety. As the saying goes, you cannot fatten the pig on the way to the market.

In this book I am going to do two things to tackle this question about the future. In the next three chapters, I will explore some of the self-soothing cultural promises that our secular society makes to ease its anxieties. Such things as the idea that secular governments, armed with progressive ideas, can forge deep communities that celebrate and cultivate deep diversity. Or the idea that as we jettison old-world faith values, society has a suitable replacement that will provide meaning and purpose beyond self-gratification. While showing that human-derived ideas will ultimately fail, I also want to encourage us to see that the Bible offers a better and truer vision of human flourishing, and can actually achieve the deepest hopes of our culture (albeit with biblical caveats). There is a biblical vision of what life is about and what its purpose is, and it is deeply satisfying! Think of this part of the book as repair work, if you like— clearing the rubble of a cultural program that is destined to fail and establishing an alternative foundation.

In the remaining chapters, we will explore a positive vision of where the church can lead the way. It's not simply the case that Christianity can outdo the secular culture, beating it at its own game; it's also that we have better things to offer the world, grounded in a certain hope about what the future will look like. So, the four chapters in this section will focus on the practicalities. We will explore how to foster a flourishing vision of life in a community that takes the cultural malaise seriously but responds with gospel joy. We'll explore how to flourish as public citizens in the culture wars when post-Christian society is so hostile to our ethics.

Our aim is not to win every argument to soothe our anxieties. Nor is it to retreat from the public square, blocking our ears to the cries of our neighbours. Our aim is to become a non-alarmed community that trusts in God because he is in control. Not so that we can say "I told you so" to those losing their heads in the cultural churn, but so that we offer a viable and attractive alternative that has our kind King at its centre.

My last book, *Being the Bad Guys*, was designed to explain how we got to where we are today. *Futureproof* is designed to explore where we are going in the future and what to do about that now. Be assured, the future will contain a vast swathe of people who have no clue about the gospel, who have never attended a church or religious ceremony, and who have no knowledge about the history of the church, its role in the formation of our culture and its norms, and why the loss of that knowledge and those norms may be problematic. Many even have no rationale for why they reflexively believe half of the things they do, or even why their conscience continues to be pricked long after the wider culture has stopped scolding them for behaviours it no longer considers transgressive. Yes, Western culture may never have been more hostile, but it has never been more open either, and both hostility and openness are set to increase. Our challenge, and our opportunity, lies in that paradox.

All of this is to be undertaken in the context of the church. Our hope should be a leaner, more humble community that is futureproofed: ready for whatever the future holds and nimble enough to adapt, yet robust enough to stand firm in a constantly changing culture.

2. Out-Purpose the Culture

It was no wonder protesters turned up in droves at the court, angry and despairing. It had taken years for women to win autonomy over their bodies in the Western world, and suddenly, at the stroke of a pen, those wins were seemingly being put into reverse. At least, that was how the protesters saw it. After all the hard-won battles over voting rights, employment discrimination, the right to divorce, and an increasing awareness of the horrors of domestic abuse, the decision by the US Supreme Court to overturn *Roe v Wade* in 2022 was seen as the first move by a government to play out *The Handmaid's Tale* in real time. Personal agency was at risk.

In a photo that went viral, pro-abortion protester Amanda Herring stood in front of the court, her full-term pregnant belly bared, with the words "Not a Human Yet" written across it in large, black capital letters. It was her way of getting the message across to the majority conservative court: *Keep your hands off our bodies!*

Yet, strangely, Herring's defiant act was seen by some of her fellow pro-choice campaigners as a bridge too far, with a Reddit discussion calling her out for, of all things, aiding the anti-abortion cause.[4] Somewhere along the line, though no one could say for sure when, that foetus *had* turned into a baby. So, surely there were two bodies in the picture now? In that moment, the mantra of a whole 50-year movement ("My body, my choice") did not seem so clear cut—even if that was only for a brief window of time. Amanda Herring's decision to unilaterally declare her freedom over her own body, one day before her due date, was being questioned even by her fellow campaigners. It turns out that when it comes to personal bodily autonomy—the right to do what we wish with ourselves—some grey areas still remain.

But not many. The raft of people voicing their concern over Herring's stunt were primarily worried about the damage being done to the pro-choice movement. Their backlash simply highlights the fact that only something as shocking as Herring's declaration can jolt people out of the conviction that we are only ever autonomous agents. The reflexive belief of our modern society is that the individual has a right to choose their own path—and that this trumps all other considerations.

We Belong to Ourselves

Western society promises us that we can find ultimate meaning and purpose as we look within ourselves. Self-discovery—finding our authentic self—can provide us with every resource needed to achieve fulfilment and find purpose. Anything that restrains self-fulfilment is a threat to individual and social wellbeing. Hence the default position is to assume that we belong to ourselves, and any authority that challenges this will be met with a vociferous and hostile response.

This is played out on a continual basis in the public square. And it's why the abortion issue is such a hotly debated matter. The argument is no longer about the viability of a baby, or when a foetus becomes a human, but about the agency of the mother. A woman cannot be forced to have a baby she does not wish to have. And her right to not have that baby now trumps that baby's right to live, regardless of its viability. The same is true of the gender debate. If we belong to ourselves, then any external "You are a man because your chromosomes say you are" is imposing a gender upon you that you may not feel defines you. Similarly, don't impose heterosexual marriage on society as the only valid expression of marriage. Don't impose marital monogamy on people when polyamory is clearly satisfactory to many throuples.

Many conservatives, including many Christians, celebrated the overturning of *Roe v Wade* as a turning of the cultural tide. Yet decisions such as this will not put the autonomy genie back into the bottle. If anything, the battle for bodily autonomy will simply become more heated as the arguments move from courts to the state legislatures.

Sixty years of the sexual revolution won't go away because of the view by a majority court that no right to an abortion can be found in the US Constitution. Two hundred years of modern philosophy built upon the insistence that each human being is free to choose their own pathway, unencumbered by the bondage of institutions and communities such as family and faith, won't be reversed by this. The overturning of *Roe v Wade* is a blip on the radar in terms of how Westerners view the right to personal choice, in matters ranging from the foods they buy at the grocery store to the gender with which they wish to identify.

Or even the church they wish to attend. For if you are a Christian reading this book, then you too are steeped in the marinade of a modern belief system that encourages you to craft your own view of yourself. Choice is the cultural default, and it's hard to resist. Any threat to remove choice is viewed as an act of violence that will do damage to one's self-esteem, one's psyche, and even one's very body. The extremes of such thinking appal many Christians, yet it is not irrelevant that being a member of a church is increasingly seen as less to do with a collective decision to serve the local body of Christ and more to do with how I wish to further my own spiritual interests and the needs of my immediate family. The choice story is deeply ingrained in many Christians.

Having been a church pastor for several decades, I have seen this again and again. It's clear that one of the most dispiriting, disempowering events for many pastors is when a family leaves your church for no particular reason. Even the widely reported failure of many adherents to return to their local churches after the pandemic lockdowns cannot simply be laid at the feet of COVID. The pandemic simply revealed that for many, online church in the comfort of one's own home, on a couch with coffee and donuts, is a plausible—indeed desirable—alternative to turning up to be with other people. And if you can find a better YouTube preacher from overseas than your local preacher, then what's wrong with that?

The Social Imaginary

Thankfully this is not the majority attitude—many Christians lamented the chance to be with fellow believers over the long months of lockdowns. Yet it is a growing one. The gospel of the autonomous self is a discipleship program like no other, with a training manual as diverse as the philosophical convictions of Jean Jacques Rousseau and the latest *Toy Story* movie with its gay marriage sub-theme. There is no escape from it. It is, in the term made popular by Canadian Catholic philosopher Charles Taylor, "the social imaginary"—the only seemingly possible way that a particular society can look at its world or can literally "imagine" it. The social imaginary does not spring out of thin air but is constructed over time by the cultural conditions we inhabit, the stories we share in common in our society, the voices permitted to have a say in the public square, and the pronouncements of our courts and governments.

Online, in our work environments, at our centres of education, and within every advertising campaign, the notion of "You do you" sits at the centre of our modern Western social imaginary. All else radiates from this. Christian thinker Carl Trueman sums up the Western intellectual default with these words:

> The intuitive moral structure of our modern social imaginary prioritizes victimhood, sees selfhood in psychological terms, regards traditional sexual codes as oppressive and life-denying, and places a premium on the individual's right to define his or her own existence.[5]

Note the word "intuitive"—it's the air we breathe. Any alternative viewpoint is already behind the eight ball, because it has to be argued from a positional disadvantage. Challenging the social imaginary in a culture is the intellectual and moral equivalent of charging up a hill to try and take a machine-gun post. And I use that imagery advisedly. To challenge the West's social imaginary will gain you enemies. If we put the modern social imaginary in one corner of the ring, and in the opposing corner put the following competing social imaginary from these verses from the book of 1 Corinthians, we see the challenge:

Flee from sexual immorality. All other sins a person commits are outside the body, but whoever sins sexually, sins against their own body. Do you not know that your bodies are temples of the Holy Spirit, who is in you, whom you have received from God? **You are not your own; you were bought at a price. Therefore honour God with your bodies.**
(1 Corinthians 6 v 18-20, emphasis added)

How many triggers can be found in these verses for our progressive culture? Roll them around your brain for a while, and the next time a friend who is not a Christian asks you why you hold to the sexual ethic that you do, bring those words out. They will look at you with a mixture of pity and horror. It sounds exactly like a form of servitude—which if course it is. The spiritual, moral and social framework that leads to 1 Corinthians 6 v 20 rejects everything that our culture stands for.

But maybe that's just the apostle Paul. Maybe we should stick to the red-letter Bible and the words of Jesus. What words in particular? How about these words:

Whoever wants to be my disciple must deny themselves and take up their cross daily and follow me. For whoever wants to save their life will lose it, but whoever loses their life for me will save it.
(Luke 9 v 23-24)

Turns out Jesus and Paul were pretty much aligned! And that's where the gospel message comes into direct conflict with the social imaginary of our times. If our purpose on earth is to be the most authentic version of ourselves that we can be, then any external voice that seeks to shape us—especially one from the Bible—is not merely an inauthentic voice but a violent, unsafe and dangerous voice. Hence by listening to such a voice we risk missing out on our true purpose in life. Do you see why the arguments are so fraught?

Something's Broken

Given all this autonomy to be ourselves and find our true purpose in life with fewer and fewer social and moral impediments to trip us up along the yellow brick road, and given that we live in a society that has vast amounts of creative resources and finances to mould the narratives that shape us, we would assume that everyone is pretty much living their best lives now. Everyone must be making authentic hay while their individual sun shines, right?

Wrong! In fact, we are facing a tsunami of anxiety, especially among younger people, and especially around matters of meaning and purpose in life. Something is not working. Something is broken. The rates of worry and depression we are experiencing are off the charts.

This anxiety wave is backed up by the research. The Australian Bureau of Statistics announced that in 2022 one in five Australians was suffering from a mental-health disorder, with young women the most affected by anxiety. Dr Zena Burgess, the CEO of the Australian Psychological

Society, declared that "Anxiety is sweeping through the country at unprecedented rates across all ages, but especially children, young people and women."[6] The pandemic has accelerated what was already evident to clinicians who, even prior to January 2020, were being swamped with anxiety-related conditions, especially among younger people. This is true across many Western countries.

But what about when the authentic self you are certain is yours for the taking remains just out of reach? What if conditions external to you keep transpiring against you, frustrating your attempts at self-actualisation? It is as if authenticity is always just one purchase or one work decision or one relationship or one experience away from being fulfilled. Social media has exacerbated this with the rise of FOMO—the fear of missing out. We see the apparently better, happier, fitter and more travelled lives of those we follow and wonder where *our* good life is.

Yet in a "You do you" world, who is there to blame when it goes wrong except you? That's the catch. If the "you" you are is struggling to attain your authenticity goals, what then? Tim Keller notes:

> *The modern self is exceptionally fragile. While having the freedom to define and validate oneself is superficially liberating, it is also exhausting: You and you alone must create and sustain your identity. This has contributed to unprecedented levels of depression and anxiety and never-satisfied longings for affirmation.*[7]

And if this affirmation is not forthcoming, then you have nowhere to go except to blame others. Carl Trueman says that the "modern social imaginary prioritizes victimhood". Tim Keller puts it this way:

*Modern therapy sees individuals as being oppressed and controlled by society's expectations, roles and structures. Greater honor and moral virtue are assigned to people the more they have been victimized ... The further **down** the existing social ladder one is, the greater honor is possible.*[8]

At this juncture it's worth observing that Western culture has indeed left a trail of victims in its wake, and much of that depended on attitudes towards race, gender and sexual preference. We cannot make light of this. Part of the Christian response in our secular culture must be to acknowledge our complicity in some egregious sins and to seek forgiveness and restoration.

Yet the victimhood issue is complex. In a therapeutic culture, verbal "micro-aggressions" include such things as forgetting to use a trans person's preferred pronouns or relating to someone of another cultural background in a manner that displays a lack of sensitivity. It's possible that you could find yourself accused of acting in unsafe and violent ways towards someone when you had no intention of doing so. And while all of this can and does present us with opportunities to listen and learn from people whose experiences are different from our own, it also leads to a culture of "keeping your head down"—with people afraid to say anything just in case it causes offence. Is it any wonder that anxiety levels are where they are?

A Distinctive Community

Is there a way out of this mess? Would it surprise you to know that the solution is joining yourself to another social imaginary? A different way of thinking about the world isn't enough on its own. We must immerse ourselves in a community that shapes our practices as well as our thoughts—a community that is shaped by practices that reject self-actualisation and embrace self-denial. Say hello to the church! For that is what the church of Jesus Christ is supposed to be: an alternative social imaginary, a different way of doing life to the one on offer in the culture.

This is not some new idea. When the gospel came to the pagan world in the 1st century, it was daring and transformative. It entered the brutal, power-driven world of Rome with an ethic of loving one's enemies; forgiving those who had hurt you; caring not only for one's own sick and hurting but the sick and hurting of other families, and indeed other ethnic and social groups; and breaking down long-held divisions that pagans could not imagine being broken down.

The building of the most daring social imaginary possible, one that challenged the dominant social imaginary of Rome, is declared by the apostle Paul when he says:

*So in Christ Jesus you are all children of God
through faith, for all of you who were baptised into
Christ have clothed yourselves with Christ. There
is neither Jew nor Gentile, neither slave nor free,
nor is there male and female, for you are all one in
Christ Jesus. (Galatians 3 v 26-29)*

If there is no male or female, then what? Too often these verses are co-opted to argue about who can preach in a church building (at one end of the theological and cultural spectrum) or (at the other end) whether there is any such thing as gender anymore.

But these verses are much more than that. Indeed, they are more radical than that. Paul is not saying that distinctions don't exist; he is saying that they are no longer the determining boundaries and distinctions for us. Our race, social status and gender are of less import than our identity and union with Christ.

These verses are the blueprint for the society of God's people, founded on an identity program determined by someone other than oneself—the Lord Jesus. To reduce these verses to my own personal autonomy push is to fail to see how radical they are. They are nothing less than a call for an alternative community that possesses a different set of values and that will create an alternative social imaginary. Wherever the church is, it offers something different to what the surrounding culture is offering. At least, it should.

In the midst of cultural anxiety and the turmoil we see facing those who are struggling to find their truly authentic selves, the church is called to be a distinctive community whose identity has been determined by dint of being in Christ.

We are called to be a forgiving community because God, in Christ, has forgiven us. I've personally, and painfully, seen that happen when my mother, along with her church friends, forgave my father for leaving her years before— years that were a financial and emotional struggle. But she offered costly forgiveness when he asked her for it.

The church is also called to be a community in which each member bears one another's burdens. I've seen, for example, church members buy cars for young refugees who had found employment but had no means of getting to the worksite.

The church is called to be a welcoming community that, instead of being self-serving, seeks to serve the interests of others. When a grandparent from a family at our local primary school died, the family was astonished at how their Christian friends were the ones leaving meals on the porch or offering to drive the children to school. It would seem as if the gospel message says that there is no room in the church for the self-fulfilment or the self-authenticity project.

Which of course is exactly what the gospel message is saying!

Denying Yourself to Find Yourself

Let's go back to those famous words of Jesus again:

> *Whoever wants to be my disciple must deny*
> *themselves and take up their cross daily and follow*
> *me. For whoever wants to save their life will lose it,*
> *but whoever loses their life for me will save it.*
>
> *(Luke 9 v 23-24)*

The very commencement of disciple life is the life of self-denial. It isn't in the fine print at the back of the contract. Jesus puts it up front and centre, and then dares us to take that step. And in every society throughout space and time in which his gospel has been proclaimed, that has proved to be a challenge.

Why? Because the self-authenticity project isn't a complete failure. Social media is full of people who are living their best lives now, doing what they wish to do now, identifying how they want to identify now, and loving it, along with their hundreds of thousands—if not millions—of followers. If you are immersed in the Western social imaginary and you have at your fingertips time, money, education, health and opportunities, then it's a pretty good ride—for now.

Conversely, if you are a struggling Christian and you have non-Christian family members who seem to be going quite well and enjoying life without God, then the gospel might not be enough to keep you—if you are only focused on the "now".

But Jesus' words are also a comfort. Do you notice how Jesus doesn't simply call for virtuous struggle for the sake of it? It's not simply about living an ethically good life. Jesus' statement is actually highly transactional. There is a reward, and there is a warning. The warning is of a lost life. The reward is a saved life. Jesus actually offers in reality what the self-authentication project promises but increasingly fails to deliver.

Of course, there's a catch too. You have to give up the self-authenticity project in order to truly gain your life. Jesus' call is a call for him to be master of your life, and for you not to be. It's a big call, but he's not throwing it out there with a "possibly" or a "maybe". He's saying that if you do it, you will one day gain everything!

Yet there *is* also a pay-off now. The church of Jesus is an outpost of God's kingdom. One day things will be "on earth as in heaven", into eternity—and we are a glimpse of that, albeit a flawed one. Something about the way we are called to live as the church now goes with the grain of how God created the universe. And it does so in a way that, despite all the hostility directed towards the church, still seems to have emotional traction.

In a culture in which the purpose of life seems to be to find "peak autonomy", and in which every subsuming of the self for the sake of another is viewed with deep suspicion, it is quite simply weird to have a purpose which is fuelled by the service of others. In a setting in which getting rid of the negative people in your life is seen as a noble cause and the path to happiness, it's deemed too risky—stupid even—to put your own interests aside for the sake of others. Yet the aimlessness of our self-focused culture stands in stark contrast to the many hidden but rich and purpose-filled Christian communities dotted across the landscape.

Perhaps it's no surprise to note that in our increasingly anxious culture, there's a rising sense even among secular writers that there is something lacking in society, something that the church seems to offer. There's something beguiling and attractive about the way that the average community of God's people operates. People who tick "no religion" seem to like their church-going friends—envying their "through thick and thin" relationships, even as they see the institution itself (what we might call the "capital-C Church") as problematic. Somehow, for all of the perceived and real travails of the church being played out in mainstream media and social media, the people of the church still seem to be "out-relating" the people of the wider culture.

What makes this possible? It's to that issue that we now turn.

3. Out-Relate the Culture

It was supposed to bring everyone together. It was supposed to be inclusive. It was supposed to highlight how we can all be one happy community and relate to each other in ways that show how united we are. But when Australian National Rugby League club, Manly Sea Eagles, unveiled its rainbow Pride team jersey just three days out from a crucial match that would go a long way to determining whether the club would make the 2022 finals, things went awry. For the one set of stakeholders not consulted in the year-long process to bring the rainbow jersey onto the playing field was the players themselves.

If you don't know much about Rugby League, think Rugby Union, NFL and Gaelic Football combined. Oh, and with zero protective gear. It's brutal and fast. Unlike Union, it is populated by blokes who didn't go to posh schools or have law degrees to fall back on. It's also populated by many Pacific Islanders who, due to the kind of genetics that build big bones and bodies, as well as fast twitch muscles for running, find themselves hot commodities in the national game. And because it's populated by many Pacific Islanders, it's populated by many culturally conservative and Christian players. You can see where this is going.

Seven Manly players, mostly from the islands of Tonga and Samoa, refused to wear the rainbow jersey and sat out the match. That's pretty much half of the team that runs out onto the field. The media response was hot and harsh. Not every response was brutal, but even the best of the secular responses was trying to tiptoe around the issue. No one in the media wanted to come across as racially superior to "unenlightened" non-whites. Yet accusations were still made that colonial Christianity in the 19th century had blinded these poor islanders to the truth, as if they didn't have the capacity to make up their own minds on matters of faith and sexuality.

The furore split teammate from teammate. Meanwhile management tried to patch up what on the face of it looked like a Leadership 101 fail in one of the most high-profile sports in the land.

Here's what didn't happen. No one was brought together. No one felt included. No one came away thinking Australia was becoming one big, happy community. No one had any sense of unity with others who differed with them in terms of ethnicity, religion or sexuality.

When Unity Fractures

There's an increasing fascination among progressive Western nations—an increasingly frantic one too—with trying to build a workable unity among their citizens going into the future. Trying to make us all relate well to each other in spite of our deepest differences. The aim is to create a unity that is no longer based on nationalism, ethnicity or religion. These three have been tried and found wanting. No one wants fascism, racism or a theocracy.

But unity has to be based on *something*. With the old liberal framework starting to crumble, and with politics now more fractured than it has been for centuries, a lot of energy is being spent on figuring out what that something is. What is supposed to define us? What is supposed to keep us together? The modern West wants to create a united vision for humanity around the concept of deep, individualised, personal autonomy. We are supposedly going to step forward into a wonderful communal future in which each of us gets to define ourselves, over and against what anyone else thinks.

In other words, we are supposed to be united around the fact that we are all completely different. We are required to celebrate everyone's diversity.

Except, of course, we don't. Because, when one person's diversity runs headlong into someone else's, we are left flailing around, accusing each other of bigotry or some sort of phobia, or of stoking the flames of a culture war. When it comes to building a consensus of how we can relate to each other in a secular society, we are unable to cope with each other's deepest differences.

The Loneliness Epidemic

Of course, the problem is not simply at an intellectual and cultural level. The deep desire for good relationships with others and for a sense that you can belong to a community that has your back is part of what it means to be human. It's personal!

That's why private citizens form groups and associations and clubs. The measure of a society's health is how well-populated and well-run its mediating institutions are. Mediating institutions are community organisations—churches, sports clubs, hobby groups, parenting groups—established by and within communities themselves. They are the buffer between the government and the individual. If the only people who visit your neighbourhood or run events are those paid to by federal, state and local governments, the odds are that your community is collapsing.

This need for a community seems obvious to me as a Christian who leads churches and church-based organisations. But having been part of a Christian community for so long—in ways that have been deeply enriching for me and my family but also painful and hard at times—it's easy to take the presence of such a community for granted. I've learned along the way that there are many people who long for a place to relate but cannot find one.

The shrivelling of communal life in the West has been well-documented. Robert Putnam's book *Bowling Alone: The Collapse and Revival of American Community*, for example, highlights the modern-day reluctance to invest in social capital. We're just not signing up as much, or as deeply, to life together with people we don't know.

Or, to take a specific example, a 2022 article in *The Sydney Morning Herald* reported how newcomers to Australia were expressing dismay that Sydney, a place that takes pride in being welcoming, is actually a hard place to fit in and find friends.[9]

Of course, there's always an entrepreneur who can tap into such needs. One newcomer, Tam Al-Saad, decided to start a dating service—not for singles looking for a romantic partner but for people just looking for friends. Having quit his marketing job, Al-Saad is making good coin from the loneliness epidemic. He sets up his clients with three other people in a café or a bar. He charges the venues who are selling food and the social lubricants of coffee or alcohol to the suck-it-and-see friendship groups. Al-Saad has arranged meetings for more than 1,500 people—mostly women, as men seem to be reluctant to admit they are lonely.

But lonely they are. One of the groups most susceptible to suicide in Australia are men known as FIFO workers—"fly in and fly out" mine workers. Large multinational mining companies have dispensed with relocating families to remote mining towns—fewer and fewer wish to go there anyway. Life could be confronting in such towns—but at least communities would spring up, with shops, service industries, schools and friendships. FIFO dispenses with community life altogether. Miners now live for up to a month at a time in air-conditioned sea-containers. And 190 workers take their own lives every year.[10]

Meanwhile the UK's loneliness epidemic has led to the government establishing a Loneliness Ministry. The ministry's suggestions for combatting loneliness—things such as checking in with neighbours or keeping in touch with family and friends by writing or calling—seem almost obvious to a previous generation. This irony is not lost on sociologist Robert Bellah:

> Just when we are in many ways moving to an ever greater validation of the sacredness of the individual person, our capacity to imagine a social fabric that would hold individuals together is vanishing.[11]

Modern office life is shredding us. Time constraints make us view new relationships as a threat, hashtag movements make us wary of those who differ from us, and new technologies mediate our interactions with other humans. Sure, wear your Manly jersey with pride, but maybe no one else will see you in it.

Jesus and Loneliness

For all of the bad press about the church in recent years, it is the church's ability (at least theoretically) to deal with conflict through the forgiveness of the gospel that is missing from other forms of community. For relationships to be maintained—indeed, for them to strengthen and flourish over time—we need more than common external interests drawing us together. We need something deep, and something that is beyond our capacity to manufacture, because anything we can manufacture has the habit of wearing out or breaking.

The church founded by the apostle Paul in the city of Ephesus got off to a rocky start. You can read the story in Acts 19. Paul's evangelistic endeavours were working well—too well. The townsfolk were turning to Jesus and away from pagan idolatry, and this was starting to affect the local idol-manufacturing business. The manufacturers had to act. They brought charges against Paul of fracturing the city's unity—and in a sly move, the leader of the agitators, Demetrius, played the religious card:

And you see and hear how this fellow Paul has convinced and led astray large numbers of people here in Ephesus and in practically the whole province of Asia. He says that gods made by human hands are no gods at all. There is danger not only that our trade will lose its good name, but also that the temple of the great goddess Artemis will be discredited; and the goddess herself, who is worshipped throughout the province of Asia and the world, will be robbed of her divine majesty.

(Acts 19 v 26-27)

The mention of Artemis—also known as Diana of the Ephesians—fanned the flames that Demetrius had fuelled. The temple of Artemis was one of the seven wonders of the ancient world. The idol of her image was the temple's main drawcard.

This wasn't simply a case of cultural or artistic pride. Temple worship was the social glue of the ancient world that enabled economic relationships to flourish. Cultural cohesion was necessary to ensure the city hummed along smoothly and flourished financially. In Acts 19, Demetrius pulled the piety lever for self-interested economic reasons. He knew he would see the city's fortunes decline if Artemis was honoured less than she used to be and Jesus was honoured more. It's nothing personal, Paul, it's just business!

The outrage engendered by Paul's supposed discrediting of Artemis brought a united reaction—a zealous, vocal, violent, united reaction—from the mob. Like a football crowd at a derby match, they cried out for two solid hours, "Great is Artemis of the Ephesians!" (v 34). Only the city's Roman leadership and its love of good order was enough to avert a riot. Not long after, Paul left the city.

Yet, daringly, when Paul later wrote to the Ephesian church, he was not shy to pull out temple language—

using it to describe the motley crew of Christians living in the shadow of one of the ancient world's biggest tourist drawcards (2 v 19-21). It's as if Paul was saying, *I see your pagan religious community, and I raise you a better one.* The letter to the Ephesians dives deep into what only the gospel can do for relationships. In 2 v 11-17, Paul describes how Jesus' death on the cross resolved both the broken vertical relationship between God and humans and the broken horizontal relationship between humans and humans. And the key term is this: "For he himself is our peace" (v 14).

In other words, the way in which true relationships are formed, and the manner in which unity is achieved, is not through a quest by us to find some external common interests with others. It is something done *for* us by the very one who is declared to be "peace". It's not for no reason that Isaiah's famous prophecy about Jesus labels him "Prince of Peace" (Isaiah 9 v 6).

Paul's description of what happens is radical. In contrast to how our culture tries to bring differing factions together, the gospel doesn't just create a space where different people can mingle and somehow find common purpose together. What Jesus does is nothing less than a work of new creation—"one man in place of the two" (Ephesians 2 v 15, ESV). We aren't different anymore but fundamentally the same. This allows for a new level of relationship that can only be a supernatural work of the Holy Spirit. He forms an intimate bond not only between those who already have common interests but even between those who previously shared a common hostility towards one another.

But it gets really radical when Paul uses temple language to describe how this works:

> *Consequently, you are no longer foreigners and strangers, but fellow citizens with God's people and also members of his household, built on the foundation of the apostles and prophets, with Christ Jesus himself as the chief cornerstone. In him the whole building is joined together and rises to become a holy temple in the Lord. And in him you too are being built together to become a dwelling in which God lives by his Spirit. (v 19-22)*

These building stones merge and head heavenward as a living building comprising a new humanity. It's a daring claim. Paul looks at the temple of Artemis, then back at the people of God, and says, *Actually, you are where the real temple and worship work is going on in Ephesus.*

To get how preposterous this must have seemed, let's update the example a little bit. There are not grand pagan temples doing a roaring trade in the Western world these days. We worship other gods. Gods such as sport. So let me take you to Tranmere Rovers.

Tranmere Rovers is a small, struggling team in the lower leagues of English football. Their home ground is just down the road from—and in full sight of—Anfield, the home ground of the mighty Liverpool Football Club. Liverpool has great history, a huge supporter base, and a bank balance that could buy Tranmere Rovers outright many times over. Which club is the powerhouse of English football? It's obvious, isn't it? Yet it's as if Paul is saying, *Forget about Liverpool. Tranmere is where football's future lies!* Only the most ardent Rovers fan could agree.

Paul goes on in his letter to the Ephesians to unpack what relationships look like in this new living temple. The joys, the pains, the costs, the benefits. It won't be easy. But the key is this: the Ephesian Christians are not joining together for merely transactional reasons. The common interest of the Christians is to be bound together in holy love. To live distinctive lives together, showcasing the goodness of God and the sweet self-sacrifice of Jesus. And to exhibit the astounding diversity of a people who, having little in common on the surface, are bonded by their love of Jesus. These Christians are not called to *attain* a unity that they have built themselves but to *maintain* a unity that the Holy Spirit has already created (4 v 3). They will need to weather serious relational storms and deep cultural and social differences—but they already have all they need to do so (see 4 v 7-16).

The Community That Out-Relates

Every church is a spiritual Tranmere Rovers. Regardless of the size of your congregation or the relative influence of your church, you're not the main game in town. Secular institutions are not looking to the church to fill relational gaps or supply meaning and purpose for society.

Yet while the stats show that fewer and fewer people identity with the Christian faith, the seeds of renewed interest may already be sprouting. A new generation, unfamiliar with church—and hence carrying little baggage—is rising. New York author and novelist Tara Isabella Burton is one of the new breed of Christians freshly discovering the radical nature of the gospel:

> *One of the many odd things about Christianity is that it trades not in grand narratives but in their subversion. Christ the king comes into Jerusalem on an ass. An ass!*[12]

So young people still become Christians. Great stuff! But this is not a time to get cocky or ferret around to find statistics to prove we're going ok. It's time to press into what it means to be Tranmere Rovers!

And a good way to do that is to plough through the likes of Ephesians and ensure that as Christian communities we are putting in place what the Bible is calling us to. In many churches there has been a dearth of what Paul calls for in Ephesians 4 v 1-2—humility, gentleness and patience. At a time when churches have ripped themselves apart over political and cultural differences (seen in the schisms over masks and mandates during the pandemic, or in the voting patterns of people from different sociological backgrounds), it's going to take effort to maintain the unity of the Spirit in the bond of peace. But the fact that Paul commands this means that he believes that God empowers us to do so.

For some churches, there will be repair work to be done. It's not simply external political or secular cultural forces that can rend us apart. Let's not underestimate how squabbles over issues such as which version of the Bible to use, what style of songs to sing (the so-called worship wars), or whether church is primarily for Christians or is supposed to be "missional" (why can't it be both?), have not simply caused division and anger but have exposed the division that is already there. Our unity often stands on very shaky ground.

But Paul goes on to describe what will grow the body up in love: "unity in the faith and in the knowledge of the Son of God" (v 13). What this means is that right and true doctrine, taught faithfully week by week and house by house, is actually the way in which a truly loving and mature community of Christians will grow. Now is not the time to go light on doctrine because of the mistaken belief that Christians don't need it any longer, or the view that people will be put off by weekly Bible teaching instead of topical sermon series that focus on felt needs. Nor is it the time to focus on the culture wars from the pulpit, as if somehow getting our man or woman into the seat of political power is the answer to what ails us.

There are two sure-fire ways to fracture your church and break its presence as a vibrant community. One is to ignore the *means* of sound doctrine that is laid out in Scripture. Whatever the churches of the future will need in an age when the secular gospel sounds so plausible, they will certainly require a solid base of biblical teaching, steeped in history and aligned with the deep, orthodox truths of the faith. Mature Christians who have fed deeply on God's word will be a strong corrective to the beguiling but false gospel of secular culture.

But secondly, churches will fracture and break if the means of sound doctrine does not lead to the *goal* of sound doctrine: the body of Christ building itself up in love (Ephesians 4 v 11-12). People are looking for a place to be loved. Unloving, uncaring, socially distant churches are a contradiction, and even more so if they are all of those bad things listed above, yet the pastor still manages to produce a banger of an exposition every week. The means and the goal go together. Maturing, loving Christians in community together is the end product.

And what are the marks of such a community? Ephesians helps us here too: holiness and righteousness. That's in Ephesians 4 and 5. If God has saved us in Christ, then a life that puts sexual sin, greed, impurity and deceitful desires aside should be the goal.

Speaking of such, how do we collectively deal with the issue of greed when it's such a cultural blind spot? We tend not to probe each other's spending habits in church, other than saying, "If you've got money, give to ministry". What would a commitment to even out financial disparities among congregants look like in church? Are we mature enough to ask a brother or sister if taking a more complex job that requires more hours and a possible relocation is necessarily the best move for their godliness, or for the church? I say this carefully, but unity has to look like something, right?

Then there's forgiveness. The watching world struggles to do forgiveness at any level. It's a cancel culture. But imagine a church in which, when we get it wrong, we don't have to cancel anyone or leave the community and find another one because sorting out the problem is too hard. What if we neither hid our sin nor held the sins of others against them, but in both instances sought confession and redress?

What if we decided to "drip-filter" Bible verses to each other during the week to encourage each other? What if we asked questions such as "How is that relationship going with the colleague who you are attracted to?" or "How can I help you with the bitterness you feel towards your mother?" Individualised piety is not our calling. Growing together as a holy temple is.

Throughout the letter to the Ephesians, we see the possibilities. Indeed, what is striking about the New Testament letters is just how practical they are and how realistic about how communities truly flourish. There's no sense of being satisfied with an outward uniformity that hides dysfunction and discord.

I want the church to be what I call "repellently attractive". I want our communities to be a conundrum to the watching society. Sure, they may be repelled initially by the fact that we won't sign up to the cultural unity ticket or march in the rainbow parade. But when tough times come, meals will be made for those who are suffering or lonely. Husbands and wives will demonstrate a love for each other that belies their circumstances. Workers will be faithful and humble, never clocking off when they shouldn't or belittling others for the sake of their own gain. When those things happen, a teeny bit of envy will seep into those watching.

Jesus is our peace. If we can build our foundation on the unity given to us by the Spirit of God, then we can out-relate the culture that we live in. When it comes to unity in the church, the sky's the limit!

4. Outlast the Culture

January 6th, 2020. The day is etched in the minds of millions of people, not simply Americans. Supporters of President Donald Trump stormed the Capitol in Washington in a protest seen by many as a challenge to the very democratic roots of the nation. But as far as this flotilla of right-wingers were concerned, it was correct to be enraged: their hopes and dreams of a better America—where freedom and agency of the individual could flourish—had been dashed.

June 24th, 2022. The day is etched in the minds of millions of people, not simply Americans. Rumours were finally confirmed that the Supreme Court of the United States of America had overturned *Roe v Wade*. Thousands took to the streets of Washington, protesting outside the court. It seemed that their hopes and dreams of a better America—in which every woman had freedom and agency over her body—had been dashed.

Here's the irony. While both groups are as far from each other on the political and cultural spectrum as they could be, they are both driven by the desire for a future in which their nation will be a better, more liveable one for everyone. A future nation in which bad ideas and bad people (those ideas and people on the other side) are either diminished or altogether banished from the mainstream.

Each group has a vision for a future society that does not include the other. A liberal democracy in which people should learn to live with deep differences is no longer an attractive idea to many people. Why would you live side by side with the 21st-century equivalent of a Nazi? Why would you share ideas with a person who feels perfectly comfortable with the deaths of 63 million unborn babies? To acquiesce is to give in to tyranny, surely!

Each side believes it is fighting for a better future. Each side is fighting against the risk of an unbearable future. Each side increasingly believes that extreme conditions will increasingly require extreme actions. And each side believes that with the right conditions and sufficient access to power it can achieve its aim of outlasting the other. None of which sounds like peace in our time.

We're All Manhattan Now

Lest my readers in the USA wonder how relevant these specific and painful domestic political troubles are to the rest of the West, let me assure you, they are! The day

Roe v Wade was repealed, articles and pronouncements across the Western world denounced the decision. The Supreme Court of Australia was called upon to seal the deal on such rights. The French president, Emmanuel Macron, declared that abortion was a fundamental right for women, while his country's legislature moved quickly to enshrine such rights constitutionally. New Zealand's prime minister, Jacinda Ardern, called the decision "incredibly upsetting". Never mind that the decision had zero legal effect in these other countries—it was about the "feels".

When it comes to the direction many in the West wish to go, it's Republican Red and Democrat Blue that are the defaults. It's not just economically true that when America sneezes the rest of the world catches a cold—it's true of our social imaginary also. Given the cultural reach of the US, now aided by rapidly advancing technologies, it's fair to say we're all living in a cultural Manhattan now.

That simply means that the deep undercurrents of popular culture, produced by the powerhouses of Disney, Silicon Valley, and, yes, Manhattan, are the long-term shapers of our thinking and our acting across the West.

And this is regardless of who wins political office. The surface conditions may change, but the cultural undercurrents are directing us all. It was the conservative political parties in the UK and Australia, not the liberal ones, who introduced same-sex marriage, after all. It seems to be clear that the progressive, individual-focused vision of what human flourishing looks like is on the ascendency, regardless of the party holding the reins of power.

Meanwhile there is almost a quasi-religious aspect to political debate in the West. It's not just a battle between right and wrong or poor thinking versus better thinking. Now the goal is for good to outlast evil, and the forces of darkness to outlast the forces of light.

A Functionally Godless Future

Why is this? Can I suggest that the primary problem is that we have bought the lie—subliminally or otherwise—that politics is, in effect, god? The new order of secular politics is spoken of in religious terms, even as the voice of religion itself fades from, or is banished from, the public square.

English author Douglas Murray has pointed out that the loss of Christianity in the West means that there is no safety net below us. If we fail and need forgiveness, we are judged by a graceless cancel culture and destined for a bottomless fall. But without God, there is no safety net *above* us either! Without that sense of a higher power, the categories and terms we once used to describe religious life start to be transferred to politics. People begin to think that there is no ceiling, no self-imposed limit, to how far our political ideology can take us or what vision it can enact. If there's no God to do things for us, it has to be the government we look to.

Politics has become our new transcendence. Political opponents are akin to reprobates and sinners; politicians are the new priesthood; the election of our political enemies will usher in hellish conditions, and the election of our political saviours will usher in nirvana.

The irony, of course, is that although we often have a sharp perception of the failings and limitations of our political and cultural opponents, that lens becomes opaque when it's turned towards ourselves. Take Scottish comic-book creator Grant Morrison, who is responsible for some of today's most creative superhero storylines. He made this comment about the possibilities of the human race:

> *We are the hands and eyes and ears, the sensitive probing feelers through which the emergent, intelligent universe comes to know its own form and purpose. We bring the thunderbolt of meaning and significance to unconscious matter, blank paper, the night sky. We are already divine magicians, already supergods. Why shouldn't we use all our brilliance to leap in as many single bounds as it takes to a world beyond ours, [since ours is] threatened by overpopulation, mass species extinction, environmental degradation, hunger, and exploitation?*[13]

In a world in which the traditional idea of God is dead, or at least on the wane, Morrison's statement bristles with optimism about humanity's capacity to choose the right path. But this is deeply naïve. Has Morrison forgotten that this same commitment to the idea of the heroic *Ubermensch* ("overman") drove Friedrich Nietzsche to insanity and Adolf Hitler to mass murder? It's not human brilliance that's the problem—it's the fractured visions our brilliance is inevitably directed towards.

Of course, most governments today aren't Hitler. My local government authority uses its power to constantly put out pamphlets and online material urging us to be good citizens and look after the planet through recycling and water-wise gardens. Sure, there's an almost liturgical framework in how these are written—authorities are cited, moral pronouncements are made, and visions of a glorious future for the neighbourhood are proclaimed. But I'm pretty on board with this particular human endeavour.

Yet at the same time, progressive governments are clamping down on religious organisations whose vision of human dignity does not accord with secular materialism. An Australian Catholic hospital that did not offer abortions or euthanasia was taken over by the state government, with little to no consultation. The local Australian Medical Association head claimed that medicine needed an approach "without being bound by ideology".[14] Meanwhile faith-based schools whose sex-education programs preference a traditional or orthodox perspective are under pressure, with legislation calling for open employment that does not take the sexual practices of staff into consideration.[15]

Not long after he lost the Australian Federal election in 2022, another Morrison, the former Australian prime minister—Scott—preached at a large Pentecostal church here in my home city of Perth. Afterwards he was pilloried by the secular media for stating that the kingdom of God is not beholden to politics. Here's what he said:

> *God's kingdom will come. It's in his hands. We trust in him. We don't trust in governments. We don't trust in the United Nations, thank goodness. We don't trust in all these things, fine as they may be and as important as the role that they play.*[16]

The very media critics who had spent his years in government warning of an approaching theocracy akin to Gilead in Margaret Atwood's *The Handmaid's Tale* were aghast. They had previously had concerns around Scott Morrison's conservative Christian convictions on matters of sexuality and his perceived lust to hold onto the reins of power. Yet suddenly they had a problem with him holding to a much looser—and lower—view of the government's role and its ability to change society. Many wondered if it was just sour grapes.

Whatever one thought of Scott Morrison's politics in Australia, it was clear that he was committed to the "safety net above": a world in which humans are answerable to a higher power. In that commitment he was much like the queen. Indeed, Archbishop Justin Welby said this at her funeral:

Jesus—who in our reading does not tell his disciples how to follow, but who to follow—said, "I am the way, the truth and the life". Her late Majesty's example was not set through her position or her ambition, but through whom she followed.

It turns out that the safest leaders are actually followers. The deep and righteous desire to shape a good future and a vision for human flourishing will inevitably go sour outside of any humbling religious restraint. A god-free heaven so often turns out to be hell on earth.

Waiting for a Godly Future

Could any orthodox Christian over the past 2,000 years have any problem with anything in Scott Morrison's statement? It looks like political theology 101, especially in light of New Testament letters such as 2 Peter. Whatever one makes of his political abilities or vision, Morrison's eschatology would look perfectly at home in most evangelical churches around the world (although, as I stated above, that mood seems to be changing).

The gospel offers us a safety net above. It keeps us from trying by force to bend others to our vision of the future, as if this world is all that we have. The letter of Hebrews says that we are "receiving" a kingdom (12 v 28)—offering a corrective to the many political ideologies that are intent on creating one.

Christians should pray for secular leaders and seek the

common good in as many areas as they can. So we can (and, in my opinion, should) be involved with politics. But the heavenly kingdom we are receiving is to be our hope and the primary focus of our energies. If that's the case, we won't tend towards despair or cynicism when the electoral cycle goes against our desires. Nor will we tend towards triumphalism or mere cultural optimism when it goes the way we want it to.

A Call to Remember

In 2 Peter 3, the apostle refocuses the Christians scattered throughout the Roman Empire (a truly transcendent-seeming political regime if ever there was one) on the kingdom that is coming to us. In effect, he tells them, *Hold your nerve. You will outlast this present age.* Peter does three things in this chapter. First he calls the church to remember:

> *Dear friends, this is now my second letter to you. I have written both of them as reminders to stimulate you to wholesome thinking. I want you to recall the words spoken in the past by the holy prophets and the command given by our Lord and Saviour through your apostles. Above all, you must understand that in the last days scoffers will come, scoffing and following their own evil desires. They will say, "Where is this 'coming' he promised? Ever since our ancestors died, everything goes on as it has since the beginning of creation."*
>
> *(2 Peter 3 v 1-4)*

For the Christian today, nothing has really changed. Just like Peter's audience, we need to look to the holy prophets of the Old Testament and the apostles of the New Testament for our direction in life. But perhaps the most encouraging thing in this passage is this: in Peter's day, just as in ours, no one outside of the Christian community was waiting for Jesus to return and usher in a kingdom that would spell the end of their own kingdoms. In fact, they were mocking the idea.

We would do well to remember this. While the Christians were preparing themselves to think in wholesome ways by the reminder that Jesus would return, those who scoffed were, by contrast, following their own evil desires because of their earthbound attitude. They insisted that nothing would interfere with the created order and the direction of history. This, of course, would leave them free to do whatever they wanted, free of any pesky notion of external judgment. But they were wrong.

Have you noticed how Peter says that he is reminding people of what they already knew? The role of the gathered people of God has to include a constant reminding that this is not all there is. Sermon series given over completely to life here and now, without an upward turning of our emotional, intellectual and spiritual eyes, are not going to help us. In the midst of turmoil, when the political agendas of our day appear to hold sway, we need to know that ultimately they will not. Our churches need to regain the biblical framework of exile and exodus, in which, just as for Israel wandering in the desert or the Jews far away in Babylon, this world is not our ultimate home or hope. We cannot become too proud if we get to pull the levers of political power, and we cannot become too despairing if those same levers are taken from our hands. Either extreme is a possibility if we lose sight of where our ultimate home is.

A Call to Patience

Secondly, Peter calls the church to be patient:

> But do not forget this one thing, dear friends:
> with the Lord a day is like a thousand years, and
> a thousand years are like a day. The Lord is not
> slow in keeping his promise, as some understand
> slowness. Instead he is patient with you, not
> wanting anyone to perish, but everyone to come to
> repentance. (v 8-9)

The problem in the West is that the church is losing patience. Think of a mother who is patient and patient and patient with her errant toddler—until she finally snaps. (Maybe it's you!) Too many churches are that mother. The cultural toddler, with its outrageous demands on the church to change and its rejection of the church's authoritative voice, pushes and pushes. Too often, God's people snap, taking matters into their own hands if the cultural trend is not in their favour. Naked politicking from the pulpit is increasingly in vogue. Any pastor with a sizeable following can rack up hundreds of thousands of YouTube views with a theologically light, politically heavy sermon. Now it's their congregations who are the toddlers, enraged at secular culture and throwing toys out of the proverbial pram.

But toddlers can be trained. Much of the New Testament's instruction is about leading God's people away from immaturity, especially in relation to our response to the world and what it offers. Paul tells the Corinthians, "Brothers and sisters, stop thinking like children. In regard to evil be infants, but in your thinking be adults" (1 Corinthians 14 v 20). And Peter writes to the scattered churches of the Roman Empire, "Like newborn babies, crave pure spiritual milk, so that by it you may grow up in your salvation" (1 Peter 2 v 2).

Tantrums are a sign of immaturity. The more mature a congregation, the fewer its tantrums! What do I mean by a mature congregation? A church steeped in the word of God, with a grand vista in mind of Christ's salvation work and its implications, and an appreciation of the indwelling work of the Holy Spirit for ministry and life as they await the return of Jesus. That kind of church will not be so frantic about cultural upheavals. The least anxious Christians I know don't necessarily have the easiest lives in terms of hostility from the culture. But they do have a deep assurance about where their hope lies, even if this present age doesn't deliver.

Most churches are not "hot" politically, and many good

pastors *are* focused on seeing the Holy Spirit transform the lives of the congregants into the image of Jesus. But even in a good and faithful church, it's easy to become cynical in the face of the political churn. It's easy to throw up your hands and retreat to a quietism that ignores the fight going on outside our walls.

Yet we are called to honour our political leaders (Romans 13 v 1-7). By God's grace, they carry out his purpose of ordering the creation. We are to be grateful that there is a system of justice, however warped it is. We must thank God that clear political leadership—even if we profoundly disagree with it—averts chaos. Don't believe me? Try getting running water in a failed state. We are to pray for our leaders that they govern well, even if they fail to acknowledge God. And we are to be patient and wait for God's kingdom to come.

So many of our failures and sins in life are down to our lack of patience. It could be as obvious as sleeping with our boyfriend or girlfriend because we can't wait until marriage. It could be demanding that God give us healing and wealth now because we can't wait until the treasures of the age to come. Or it could be focusing hard on earthly politics—shaping all of our conversations, our friendships and our energies around it—because we've lost sight of the fact that the church of God is a real outpost of the coming global political order of King Jesus.

At the start of his letter, Peter says that God's power has given us "everything we need for a godly life" (2 Peter 1 v 3). While temporal power may hold out the promise of a smoother path, it is as we lean into God's power that the change we actually need—change within ourselves—truly comes.

A Call to Holiness

Finally, Peter calls the churches to be holy:

> Since everything will be destroyed in this way, what kind of people ought you to be? You ought to live holy and godly lives as you look forward to the day of God and speed its coming. That day will bring about the destruction of the heavens by fire, and the elements will melt in the heat. But in keeping with his promise we are looking forward to a new heaven and a new earth, where righteousness dwells. So then, dear friends, since you are looking forward to this, make every effort to be found spotless, blameless and at peace with him. (3 v 11-14)

The primary focus of the church is to be holiness and godliness! There is an assumption here from Peter that the place for holy, godly behaviour is never going to be the culture we live in. The church is going to be part of the new heaven and the new earth, and the old politics won't make it through to the other side. How do we know? Because Peter tells us that in that new setting, "righteousness dwells". A number of other translations, including the NRSV and the Good News Bible, put it in a lovely way: "where righteousness is at home". It gives the impression of righteousness feeling "at home" in a "Hey, I like it here, this fits me!" kind of way.

Which politics will feel at home in the new creation? Leftist politics? Centre-right? Hard-right? None of the above. The politics of a holy, godly gathered people of King Jesus will feel at home there. The people of God who have shaped their lives in this age by the sure and certain hope that the political elements of this world, as well as the physical elements, will melt in the heat. That's who will feel at home there.

The call of the gospel is for the church to outlast the culture—not simply because it can but because it will! The question for us is: will we make the most of that outlasting? We need a deep conviction that King Jesus is calling us to a holy, patient life of remembrance. A deep interest in and commitment to our eschatological hope is not defined by the end-times charts we embrace or the "prepper" bunkers we own, but by godly lives of hope centred around the total victory that Jesus will bring to his people. We've been saved, beyond what we deserved; it's now our responsibility to live spotless, unblemished and peaceable lives before a watching world.

Now of course that can and will involve politics. I know a number of fine politicians who are followers of Jesus. And because politics is part of our world, and because— as former Dutch Prime Minister and theologian Abraham Kuyper said—"There is not a square inch in the whole of creation over which Christ, who is Sovereign over all, does not cry: 'Mine!'",[17] we don't vacate the public square, especially in the political world. Whether it's grassroots community service, advocacy for the repressed, or high-level political engagement, we are all able to engage in political acts, doing good to the "polis"—the city or state. And we can promote the goodness of the gospel along the way.

A Truly Transcendent Future

My theological conviction is that the gathered church of Jesus Christ in a local expression is the template—albeit an imperfect one—of future reality. It will outlast every other gathering, every other political framework, every other idea about what the future might look like. The church will outlast it all. And if that's the case, then it's not a waste of time pouring our time and energy into it. The gates of hell, Jesus said, will not outlast the church (Matthew 16 v 18)—whatever seems to be the case in the present.

The Bible encourages each other to keep meeting together—"and all the more as we see the Day approaching" (Hebrews 10 v 25). The impending end of the age and the travails we experience are not an excuse to dial down our commitment to God's gathered people, but a reason to dial it up. In the face of countless political movements that posit a godless future, Christians can offer one in which God, the Creator, Saviour and Sustainer of all, is at the centre. That's the only good future that will truly last.

5. Polarisation: How to Flourish as a Community

My wife and I enjoy decompressing by watching the YouTube series *Apartment Therapy*. And therapy it is! Various funky apartment-dwellers showcase their stuff: their furniture, their art, their quirky purchases and their lifestyle choices. Sitting with a glass of wine at the end of a busy week, it's hard not to envy those who curate their apartments to reflect their interesting lives. Their interesting *single* lives. For almost everyone featured on *Apartment Therapy* lives alone. Not alone in the proverbial "cat lady" sense, surrounded by the sad vestiges and overstuffed packing boxes of bad choices. But alone in a self-actualised way. Alone as the pinnacle of their self-crafted achievements. There's no sense for most that this is a pitstop on the way to living with more people in the future.

Greater and greater numbers of people in the West now live alone. UK government statistics in 2021 revealed that the number of people living alone had increased by more than eight percent in ten years. As for the US, former director of the United Nations Population Division Joseph Chamie observes:

> *America is in the midst of a transformation in household living arrangements with one in seven adults now living alone, amounting to more than one-quarter of all U.S. households. It's time to fully recognize the historic transformation of America's households and adapt to its far-reaching social, economic and political consequences.*[18]

And it's not all *Apartment Therapy* or that serendipitous find at the flea market. The UK government has established a Commission of Loneliness. Without social capital, alone time becomes lonely time.

This has implications for our wellbeing. Author and pastor Sam Allberry writes that non-sexual "cuddling services" are now available for people who have been starved of human touch.[19] We're outsourcing the almost incidental interactions that humans need and that so many of us take for granted.

The Polarised Life

This trend is confronting enough on its own, but it isn't just that. People are not merely physically separating but politically, culturally and psychologically too. We're *polarising*: cutting ourselves off deliberately from folk we don't agree with. If we never bump into, shop with, or do work with anyone who thinks differently to us, we are on the path to isolationism. Allberry observes:

> *If physical presence is a way of honouring our humanity, it is also sadly true that we can all too easily dehumanise those we are not physically around.*[20]

The city of Belfast in Northern Ireland, where I was born, is a case in point. For decades Catholics and Protestants have been literally divided from each other by "peace walls"—high fences that still run through the centre of the most divided areas. Even since the Good Friday Agreement in 1998, which ended most of the violence of the Troubles, it has not proved easy to shift back to living alongside those with whom you disagree. Tensions rumble along.

With politics seemingly the new religion in our post-Christian age, sectarian divisions are increasing. Now many young people in the USA are forgoing the annual pilgrimage home for Thanksgiving. The alternative to a door-slamming argument with Uncle Max, who came to dinner in his MAGA hat? Stay put and do Thanksgiving with friends who think like you do. No need to adjust or restrain yourself in the face of difference.

Yet this self-crafted life, in which we avoid the niggles and irritations of putting up with others, is biting us hard.

Cutting ourselves off from each other is not the pathway to authentic, flourishing humanity.

Gospel Social Animals

As we move forward, let me remind you of the implications of this book's first section: the gospel gives us a better vision for the future than the world can offer. It contains a better hope and a better purpose. And it wraps up all of this in a vision of a new humanity, shaped by the very God who created us in the first place. Building on this, in the next four chapters we are going to examine four areas of anxiety that are eating up secular culture—polarisation and loneliness first, and then technology, culture wars and ecology—and ask how Christians can respond healthily and robustly. The Bible has things to say about all these topics! And if we put its commands into practice, we will become that non-anxious structure I talked about in the first chapter, able to provide respite and hope for those who are battered and bruised by the world's flawed vision of human flourishing.

So, first up: let's embrace community.

It's been said that humans are "social animals", but the radical truth about the church is that we are *gospel* social animals. As we saw in chapter 3, we've been brought together not by our common interests but by the Holy Spirit. Our job is to "maintain [not attain] the unity of the Spirit through the bond of peace" (Ephesians 4 v 3). What we cannot do, God has done. That's powerful!

Yet even in the church, polarisation lurks. COVID-19 exposed deep divisions. Christians refused to take each other's differences in good faith. And in hot political times, the trend for churches to divide along party lines has soared. How you vote can be a bigger factor in deciding where to go to church than good theology or the needs of brothers and sisters in your current congregation.

The "Great Reset" that affected work life post-COVID also affected church. Worshippers didn't merely decrease their attendance—many checked out altogether. Others decided that online Christianity was the future. Church in the metaverse, anyone?

The New Testament presents this as neither desirable nor viable. God's word does not recognise a self-actualised, individualised Christianity in which authenticity is found in personal autonomy. It doesn't have much time for the polarised, ornery Christian who can't get on with anyone else and separates over minor issues. Instead, the Bible uses the language of the body—one body—to describe our interconnectedness.

The communal life of Jesus' followers described in the Bible comforts and challenges us. It comforts those who feel lonely and isolated and without social capital, because it shows that deep connectedness is more than possible in Christ. And it challenges the self-satisfied *Apartment Therapy* philosophy—in which anything or anyone that doesn't fit our preconceived ideas about personal flourishing is passed on to the thrift shop—because it tells us that following Jesus pretty much *has* to involve other people, including people who are very different to ourselves.

Community Life in Crete

Paul's letter to Titus is a great example of doing relationally rich life together as God's people. And it's helpful as we discuss polarisation, because the wider societal life of Crete (where Titus was working among the churches) seems to have been toxic, to say the least. Crete had a reputation for exhibiting some challenging behaviours: the words "lazy", "liars" and "brutes" come to mind (Titus 1 v 12)! Paul's description of Crete makes it seem like a cheap package-tour island of personal pleasure. Yet he wanted to ensure that the Cretan church "hit different" to the rest of the island's inhabitants.

The surrounding cultural chaos and relational debris did not have to define the church. Paul instructed Titus to shape an alternative Cretan community. This change was focused on Christians and would only be possible by the power of the gospel—yet it would also be good for the whole society. Paul's instructions to bondservants, for example, aimed to ensure "that in every way they will make the teaching about God our Saviour attractive" (2 v 10).

Selfless Self-Control In a Selfish Society

Paul's instructions to Titus were designed to pull the Cretan Christians back from the selfishness of the society around them. For those who had decided to follow Christ, a new way of living was required. In fact, a new "self" was required—one that was shaped by the needs of others, not just one's own desires. One that enabled and enriched community life.

Paul wanted Titus to teach "sound doctrine" (2 v 1), but this was no dry theology; it was practical. Self-control and selflessness were to be at the heart of the church:

> *Teach the older men to be temperate, worthy of respect, self-controlled, and sound in faith, in love and in endurance. Likewise, teach the older women to be reverent in the way they live, not to be slanderers or addicted to much wine, but to teach what is good. Then they can urge the younger women to love their husbands and children, to be self-controlled and pure, to be busy at home, to be kind, and to be subject to their husbands, so that no one will malign the word of God. Similarly, encourage the young men to be self-controlled.*
>
> *(v 2-6)*

Older men, older women, younger women and younger men: the common requirement for all four groups of people that Titus had to disciple was the quality of self-control. (In the case of the older women, Paul uses the word "reverent" instead, but follows it up with "not to be slanderers or addicted to much wine", which sounds like self-control to me; it's a prohibition against uncontrolled drinking and an uncontrolled tongue.) The term "self-controlled" appears again in verse 12. It's also used in the list of attributes to be held by an elder in Titus 1 v 8.

Self-control just didn't seem to be a Crete thing, at least among the pagans. Self-indulgence was more their schtick. Yet in the Spirit-enriched community of the church, godly self-control was to be the gravity that held together all sorts of relationships. I'd commend reading through the whole letter—it's brief and punchy. You'll see that orbiting this central quality of self-control are other personal and communal virtues (faith, love, steadfastness, hospitality, submission to authorities, gentleness towards others, courtesy). Self-control, and the lack of it, has a profound impact on our relationships with one another.

We can see the truth of this in so much of the isolation, polarisation and loneliness in our Western communities today. A lack of sexual self-control splits up marriages and families. A lack of emotional self-control when dealing with errant neighbours or people who let you down (or cut in in traffic!) leads to embittered relationships with even the most trivial acquaintances. A lack of physical self-control leads to the anger and violence that drives women into refuges. The absence of this fruit of the Spirit (Galatians 5 v 23) has profound negative implications for society.

When Self-Control Goes Bad

It's worth adding that the seemingly good can actually be just as selfish as uncontrolled and dissolute lifestyles.

We may get up early, train in the gym or run hundreds of kilometres, eat a strict diet, work hard and for long hours, remain disciplined in our sex lives, seek financial security and write strict budgets. But this form of self-control can be just as isolating and as toxic to others as the Cretan lifestyle can be. We can be sexually pristine, drug-free, bodily toned, financially and relationally successful and utterly, utterly selfish—never concerned to put ourselves out for the sake of others.

Nowhere else has the self been elevated like it has today the West. Even self-care has been hijacked. Cultural commentator Tara Isabella Burton says:

> The idea of self-care ... is now often used to frame
> individual pleasurable actions, like taking a bubble
> bath or cancelling plans, as morally worthy, even
> necessary ... According to this newly prevalent
> gospel of self-actualization, the pursuit of private
> happiness has increasingly become culturally
> celebrated as the ultimate goal.[21]

I do not want to diminish a healthy understanding of self-care. There are times when we need to de-frag and take the foot off the pedal of relational engagement. Even Jesus did this, and he instructed his disciples to do so too (Mark 6 v 31). But it was always about being refreshed for the tasks ahead, never the end in itself.

It's interesting that Burton uses the word "gospel" to describe the current popular idea of self-care. Because what we're dealing with is an alternative good news to the gospel of Jesus Christ. And at the centre of this new gospel is the self. It may be a dissolute self or a disciplined self, but it is always all about you! What you want, where you think things should go, what lifestyle you would most enjoy. And if someone else gets in the way of that, then you can cut them loose with a clear conscience.

Godly self-control, such as we find described in Titus, is the opposite. It is about us restraining ourselves not just for our own sakes but for the sake of other people. Self-control admits that, left to our own devices, we would not tend towards the interests of others but towards our own interests—and seeks to do better.

A lack of godly self-control—either through dissolute living or through self-focused disciplined living—can shred healthy community. But self-control for the sake of others? That's an adornment of gospel doctrine.

Self-Control in a Selfless Church

The church worships the one who exhibited self-control to the utmost and did so for the sake of others. As Paul finishes his instructions on self-control, he concludes:

> For the grace of God has appeared that offers
> salvation to all people. It teaches us to say "No"
> to ungodliness and worldly passions, and to live
> self-controlled, upright and godly lives in this
> present age, while we wait for the blessed hope—
> the appearing of the glory of our great God and

Saviour, Jesus Christ, who gave himself for us to redeem us from all wickedness and to purify for himself a people that are his very own, eager to do what is good. (Titus 2 v 11-14)

In his life and in his death, Jesus put aside his own interests for the sake of the interests of others. He lived a self-controlled life that enabled him to die a self-giving death in order to "purify for himself a people" (not just individuals!). His call is for each of us to put self-interest aside in the same way and follow his example. And he has empowered us by his Spirit to do so.

As society becomes more hostile, and the political and cultural tone more bracing, the temptation for each of us is to become our own personal pleasure island. Maybe not Crete, but perhaps Ibiza or Bali—a place of self-affirmation, self-care and self-focus. We might wrap it up in religious language, but the truth is that it is just the same old cultural discipleship program—the secular gospel. We need to turn away from that view of the world, asap. Commentator David Brooks calls out the self-consciously crafted lifestyle of *Apartment Therapy*— "selfism". Brooks wryly states:

We live in a culture of selfism—a culture that puts tremendous emphasis on self, on self-care and self-display. And one of the things we've discovered is that you can be a very good person while thinking only about yourself![22]

But the call of Christ is to exchange this supposedly noble selfism, or "higher selfishness", for a higher self*less*ness.

What does this actually look like for us? Here are some suggestions to start your exploration of that question.

A Plus-One Life

In the new church plant we attend, there's a system called "Plus One". Each term we are asked to do just one specific thing extra that adds to the life of God's people. That may be having dinner with another couple or family from church once a month. It may be regularly praying with or for one particular person in the church. It could be deliberately spending time with one non-Christian friend.

It doesn't sound like much. There's no giving everything away or holding everything in common. It isn't very "ninja Christian". This means it's workable, and it's transferable. It's "Plus One", not "Times Everything"! The Plus One idea accepts that most of life is ordinary and most of us are ordinary. But if you start with bite-sized, ordinary ways of focusing on other people, you may just hit your target.

"Adopt" the Lonely

Following Jesus can seem easier if you've got your life together. And harder if you haven't. Has your church family considered that people turning up at church might be more complex, with more baggage and less social capital, than in the past? It's easy for families to hang out with other families and do life and meals and holidays together. But what about those individuals who don't normally make the cut? What if a teenager who's grown up in tough times with a single mum came on your family holiday—and in the process got to see what it's like for younger men to respect older men or for a dad to love his children and exercise self-control in discipline? What if an older woman who experiences same-sex attraction got to be involved in your family devotions from time to time? What if a singleton who lacks community were to come round for a quick cup of tea after work once a week, or a single mother and her kids were to be routinely invited on your family days out?

This can have huge "adorning the gospel" consequences. A few years back, a lonely older man with "a past" turned up at the church I was pastoring. He lived in a hard-scrabble suburb, in the type of apartment block you see on the news. He'd done some things that he regretted and that had fractured his family. He'd been converted later in life. The commitment to him by certain men in the church and their families was stunning. He didn't become their project; he became their friend. He became included in the life of the community.

One day a year or so back, he died suddenly at home—alone. When the police found him, they checked his phone to find out who his friends were. The first people they contacted, by dint of the number of calls on his phone, were the blokes at church. We organised his funeral. We helped his family members with their grief. They were stunned when all sorts of church people—men and women, younger and older—turned up at a funeral that, if he'd had no church family, would have been very small indeed. Those men adorned the gospel with their lives.

Fostering Programs

A few years ago, when pastoring a church, I showed a short interview during the service one Sunday. It was just a two-minute video call I'd had with a young woman who worked with the Department of Child Protection. One comment she made sparked a huge change in our church. She told me that despite the huge volume of children needing to be fostered, very few Christian families got involved. God did something in our people following that video! Two families now foster on an ongoing basis, while the rest of the church has gotten involved in support—providing respite care and cooking bulk meals on a regular basis for the fostering agency to hand out to foster families across the city to make life that little bit easier.

It has become more challenging for orthodox Christian families to foster, as agencies are often suspicious of the values framework of the gospel. Proselytising is off-limits. But foster children do often end up coming along to church with their foster families, engaging with other families and children, and being given the opportunity to see a richer, deeper expression of life. They get to see the unity of the gospel in action, and—we hope—may even become part of it themselves.

Social-Media Accountability

There's a great *New Yorker* cartoon of a woman standing at the door to the study, dressed in her pyjamas, asking her husband, who is on his computer, "Aren't you coming to bed?" His reply: "I can't. There's someone who's wrong on the internet."

There's always the one Christian in your setting who is a keyboard warrior. Here's hoping it isn't you. The polarising of our society is exacerbated by our tendency to dehumanise those we don't actually come into contact with, and we are in danger of increasing this polarisation. Given the current pushback against Christianity in the West, it's easy to feel demonised by some of the searing mockery towards our faith—and to end up fighting fire with fire.

A lack of self-control in increasingly heated online arguments is a poor witness to the gospel. It's time we took a spiritual health check of how we engage with others—including other Christians with whom we disagree—online. It's fairly common practice these days, for men especially, to have an accountability partner to help with staying away from online porn. But what about online arguments? Is there a person (or a group) who has permission to stop you from piling in?

As the online world merges with the real world, there are real challenges and opportunities for God's people. We can demonstrate self-controlled lives that are sober-minded and dignified. Believe me, people will notice.

Engage with Public Life and Debate

Public discourse is more abrasive and toxic than ever. Christians are often seen as "the bad guys". So it's tempting to retreat to a personalised quietism that has little interest in public life.

This means it's more important than ever to engage in a godly manner and not be polarising in the public square. We have the opportunity to be subject to our authorities, to do good to everyone and not to slander or be quarrelsome (Titus 3 v 1-2). What might that look like?

What about contacting our local politicians to assure them we are praying for them? What about asking if there is any local problem that the church can help alleviate? At the very least, we should be praying publicly for our political leaders. If we don't, we are tacitly implying that public life is unimportant. At a time when political opponents dehumanise each other, let's humanise them all before the God who created them.

It's possible to exercise gentleness and self-control even during difficult cultural debates. Our state's main newspaper is often hostile to independent schools. One journalist wrote an article recently about why she was in favour of government education, citing her own negative experience of an independent school growing up. She began her article along these lines: "I assume I will get trolled for this, but…"

It was a thought-provoking piece with which I disagreed. I wrote to her to give her my thoughts—and to commend her bravery for stepping into the fray. Here's what she wrote back:

> *I can't thank you enough for taking the time to write an intelligent, reasonable letter about this. When I feel like I am adding to public debate, I feel like I am doing my job.*

Contrary to *Apartment Therapy*, it isn't all about *my* flourishing. It's about seeking the good of all. Sure, it seems like a small, incremental step to write an encouragement to someone with whom you disagree. But that's how these things work: incrementally—and in both directions. C.S. Lewis's idea of hell in his book *The Great Divorce* is a town in which people are constantly bickering with each other, falling out over the pettiest things. They then move further out of town. Launder, rinse, repeat for eternity. Eventually everyone lives thousands of miles from each other in splendidly devilish isolation. But not flourishing. Far from it. They're withered, angered, bickering and self-focused.

The gospel unity that we are called to maintain means wanting to see others flourish too, even if we disagree with them. And the church models this. Of course, we know that the first step to true eternal flourishing is to meet Jesus. Deep disagreements must continue with those who reject the gospel. But that doesn't mean we have to treat our opponents badly.

Godly self-control that adorns the gospel was the solution to the polarised, selfish situation on Crete—and also a witness to the gospel. Selflessness and the pursuit of unity were what made the Christians' beliefs about Christ deeply attractive. Selfless self-control is both a solution and a witness to the polarised, selfish situation in our own towns and cities too.

6. Technology: How to Flourish as a Participant

This chapter was written by ChatGPT.

Not really. But could you tell the difference? What if, on a particularly busy Friday afternoon, with a writing deadline looming, I had said to ChatGPT, "Hey, write a chapter of a book on technology and how Christians can engage with it well, in the manner of Australian blogger and author Steve McAlpine"? Would it have come up with anything different to what you're about to read? Would it be wiser? Would it be duller? Would it worry you if you couldn't tell the difference?

It seems that technology will soon not only be able to provide us with writing in the style of our favourite authors but will read it in their voice and then with their avatar. This is not just the stuff of sci-fi. When hundreds of technology luminaries, including Elon Musk, sign a letter expressing their concerns that "the world is moving too fast in adopting AI without understanding the ramifications of going big on a fundamentally different type of technology", you might pause for thought.[23] Tech gurus are calling for "time-outs" in an industry that moves at ever-increasing speed—and whose tendrils invade our lives in ways that we increasingly cannot untangle.

There was a time when the key worry about technological advances was the threat to low-skilled labour—when automatons took over assembling cars and production-line workers were put out to pasture. We've moved past that point. I get ads on Facebook now telling me that I can get blogs written better and more quickly than I can write them myself. And what if ChatGPT could one day offer you legal advice that's quicker, cheaper, and more water-tight than the family firm in your local town?

Christians on the Front Foot

We might feel like Christianity doesn't have that much to say about all of this. It feels so overwhelming and beyond the ken of all but the few in our congregations who work in IT. Christians are rightly concerned about online porn and how ubiquitous it is, so we're constantly on about accountability. But what else can we do?

Oh, we did Zoom-church during the pandemic. But now we're trying to get back to normal church. And sure, we don't like cancel culture—though we're heartened by seeing secularists share our Christian concern over freedom of speech. But there isn't always a "Christian Answer" to these issues. If our political leaders seem incapable of stopping private citizens from using our data for their own ends, what chance us? Aside from becoming Amish, what else can we really do except use technology in a way that seems moral, and avoid its excesses and dark side?

But what if Christians could go on the front foot? What if we had something to say to the surrounding culture about what it means to flourish in an online world? I believe we *are* well placed to speak into this space—with a message of deep hope and rich relationship. We have something to offer an anxious world that is increasingly disembodied—and discombobulated—by technologies that it feels have spun out of control.

First, let's explore those anxieties and get to the root of what's going on.

We Fear the Technology

AI is just one technological concern among many. If you are a younger person reading this, then you are a "digital native". There has never been a time when an online life was not your experience. For older types—"digital tourists" or "late adopters"—we're trying to figure out which parts of technology we will say yes to and which parts we will say no to. But when my Gen-X crowd dies off (or ends up in nursing homes listening to Nirvana and

Nickelback on endless rotation), it will be online tech and communications all the way down.

And it's the blurring between non-technological reality and technological reality that is causing concern. Simply put, there is no division between the two for digital natives. A social psychologist from New York University, Jonathan Haidt, has traced the spike in teenage and young-adult anxiety in the West, linking it to the huge impact of social media starting around 2012. Haidt says that, despite a generation of younger people growing up in the "everyone gets a trophy" era, the levels of insecurity are unparalleled among a cohort who have the world at their fingertips:

> *We are now 11 years into the largest epidemic of teen mental illness on record. As the [Centre for Disease Control and Prevention's] recent report showed, most girls are suffering, and nearly a third have seriously considered suicide. Why is this happening, and why did it start so suddenly around 2012?*[24]

Haidt's study shows that despite an insistence in the mainstream media that political instability is the primary driver, the common factor across all demographics is the amount of social media being consumed. Or, more poignantly, how much social media is consuming *them*.

Business leader, church planter and author, Daniel Sih, posits that one day we will look back and see that just as our lack of interest in the ills of smoking cigarettes took a heavy toll, so too will our almost casual handing over of the iPad to our two-year-olds:

> *Might it be possible, then, for future generations to look back in disbelief and ponder, "How did they not see the connection?" "Did they really not realise that video gaming made kids irritable and emotional?" "Did they really not see that learning and focus diminished with early screen use?" "Did they really not understand the impact of interactive media on the developing brain?"*[25]

Then there's porn. Big, capital-"P" Porn. Invasive, technologically advanced porn that is available 24/7 in the Babylon that our children carry around in their pockets. That *our adults* carry around in their pockets. Sex education—bad sex education—is just one click away, and always one step ahead of blockers and parental controls. Porn is no longer magazines and pubic hair. It is strangulation and violence, in 4k. And as online journal *The Conversation* states, "Longitudinal studies among adolescents find watching pornography is linked to sexually violent behaviour later in life."[26]

And how about algorithms? Any opinion you reveal by what you watch or search for online will send you down a deeper and deeper rabbit hole. The political and ethical polarisation we are experiencing is partly because of algorithms designed to show us things we want to see rather than content we might disagree with. If you think

Harry and Meghan are the best thing that ever happened to the UK royal family, you'll find your Facebook feed full of content that agrees. If you think they're the worst, you won't see anything that will try to change your mind.

Influencers for the Future

Many celebrate the shift of information control from government to private citizenry. In theory it allows more voices to be heard, and surely that's a good thing? Yet social media rewards bad behaviour. The more unrestrained and transgressive you are, the more "authentic". And authenticity is a high bargaining chip in our psychologically driven West. In response, the social-media efforts of traditional institutions are failing to keep up, and appear inauthentic.

The individual influencer is the future. Take Joe Rogan, the machismo-laden, conservative but hedonistic commentator who has almost 8 million Twitter followers and nearly 16 million on Instagram. Rogan is a disrupter in the new media age. He shapes the opinions of working-class men who feel ignored by the more progressive mainstream media. Or there's Andrew Tate, the self-appointed relationship advisor—and misogynist—whose videos have been lapped up by millions of young men, many of them schoolboys who envy Tate's way with women and his bling. You know you're getting old when you only hear of the likes of Tate when his cancellation makes the mainstream media. I asked my 14-year-old if he had heard of Andrew Tate. "Of course," he said. "Everyone knows who Andrew Tate is." Clearly!

Social media and new technologies fast-track cultural change. The first time you might hear that your daughter is gender-curious is when she tells you over dinner that it's he/him pronouns from now on. A transgender young person in hipster Portland, Oregon, can influence and converse with your teenager in outback Australia or rural South Africa tomorrow. Today, actually. Such radical ideas once took years to filter to the edges of culture. Now they move at broadband and 5G speed.

Something's in the water. And everyone is feeling it. My 50-something neighbour observed that something was wrong in the public conversation—something toxic. She didn't like the way no one was able to disagree with anyone without it becoming angry and hateful. "It feels like we've lost something that Christianity gave to us," she said. And this from someone who makes no claim to be a Christian.

Digital Discipleship

My neighbour is on to something. This *is* about discipleship. We're always being discipled by something—for good or ill, Christian or not. Discipleship is the immersive crafting over time of practices that become our default ways of living. Our digital technologies are simply high-level immersive discipleship tools. They are training us.

I once heard Tim Keller, who planted Redeemer Presbyterian Church, New York, highlight the trend in which many young Christians lose their faith within six months of leaving home to go to college. His conclusion was that the discipleship program of their church was running on "audio", while the discipleship program of the university was running on "video".

By that he meant that the university discipleship program seemed more real—more vivid and therefore more compelling. It was a deeper, more immersive and more communal experience than their church had offered them. Add the allure of cut-price sin, an introductory philosophy unit that questions the existence of God, and a non-Christian romantic partner, and then simmer for one term. Result? An ex-Christian student, and a shocked set of parents around the dinner table during the semester break.

In the decade or so since Keller made that observation, the cultural discipleship program the church is combatting has shifted up a gear. We're dealing with a discipleship program that has gone digital. Now by "digital", I don't mean the literal technological shift from video platforms to digital platforms. I'm using Keller's "how much more" logic: just as the jump from church "audio" to university "video" was a switch from a less compelling discipleship program to a more compelling one, so too in this latest shift.

Just as college's discipling program seemed sharper, clearer—more existentially satisfying and psychologically alluring—than the church program, the modern-day secular discipleship process is even more pervasive and persuasive. And that's partly because it *is* literally digital and therefore more ubiquitous. You don't go to it; it comes to you. Instagram, TikTok, Facebook, online dating apps, click-and-purchase—you name it. Or perhaps you can't name it.

My point is, the most successful discipleship is caught, not taught. The ideas and practices our culture is training us in simply become as reflexive as your arm is when it reaches for your phone first thing in the morning. Think how hard it is to stop that move. You have to have something to counter it. A counter-discipleship program!

The Stuff of Life

Which is exactly what the Bible gives us. The context of Scripture is never discipleship in a neutral setting. God's word has always provided a counter-discipleship program that seeks to be more compelling than what the surrounding cultures have to offer.

The book of Deuteronomy is God's "digital" discipleship program. It's an out-discipler! And in its first context, it needed to be. Given to God's people when they were on the verge of entering the promised land, Deuteronomy pitched a richer, deeper vision of life than the culture they would find on the other side of the Jordan River.

The problem with the land of plenty was, well, that it was a land of plenty! It was a veritable "click and purchase" milk-and-honey experience. The biggest threat to God's people as they entered the promised land was not a bad life but a *good* life that would draw their hearts away from the Giver and towards the gifts. Meanwhile, the nations they were to dispossess had alluring sexual and idolatrous practices that would seek to disciple them towards actions God had forbidden. But the aim of God's counter-discipleship program in Deuteronomy was to present a compelling vision for human flourishing under his kingship—one that would put the culture of Canaan to shame. It would be like comparing *Avatar II* with a grainy black-and-white Charlie Chaplin film featuring jangly piano music and subtitles.

The famous passage known as the *Shema* sums up God's "digital" strategy:

> *Hear, O Israel: the* LORD *our God, the* LORD *is one. Love the* LORD *your God with all your heart and with all your soul and with all your strength. These commandments that I give you today are to be on your hearts. Impress them on your children. Talk about them when you sit at home and when you walk along the road, when you lie down and when you get up. Tie them as symbols on your hands and bind them on your foreheads. Write them on the door-frames of your houses and on your gates.*
> *(Deuteronomy 6 v 4-9)*

All bases were covered. They were to start with their own hearts and then work out to the hearts of their children.

And they were to make faith in God the stuff of life. Thinking about him was not just a Sabbath day task; it had to be done at home and away, at night and when getting up. God's commands were on the Israelites' bodies and on their property. Everywhere they looked and in everything they did. That's immersive discipleship. God's commands would be the first thing their arm would reach for in the morning.

The people of God were to go "digital" from the start. They couldn't afford not to. There was no sense that they were to outsource this discipleship program to the experts or to paid staff members of a worshipping community. The law had been given to them all, just as the land had been given to them all. Who, therefore, was responsible for rolling out this discipleship program? All of them.

Written on Our Hearts

It won't surprise you when I say that the same is true for us now. Our culture is not neutral in its desires for us. The invitation remains to love things and people other than God with all of our hearts and with all of our souls and with all of our strength. And the solution to this tension is neither to give in nor to go "peak Amish".

What follows is not a list of how-tos for getting off Instagram or Twitter. It's not a series of bullet points for talking to your teens about online bullying or porn. These are important matters. But we won't out-disciple the culture by playing a reactionary game of "Whack-a-Mole" with it. If we are to futureproof ourselves from discipling technologies we cannot yet envisage, we must—and can—create a compelling counter-discipleship program that is as thick and immersive as the *Shema* was to be for Israel.

Thicker and more immersive, actually. Because here's our hope. The law that was written externally on the bodies and dwellings of God's Old Testament people has been written internally on the hearts of God's New Testament people (Hebrews 8 v 8-12; 10 v 15-18). By the power of the Holy Spirit, the discipleship program we desperately need has been internalised. We have been immersed into something that is more than able to counter what is on offer today.

So that's all good then! We can get on with living our individualised lives outside of an immersive experience, because God has immersed us in his Spirit. Well, no, actually. God's call for us to participate in an immersive discipleship community goes even deeper in the New Testament. Shortly after making the point about God's laws being written on our hearts, the writer to the Hebrews urges us:

> *Let us consider how we may spur one another on towards love and good deeds, not giving up meeting together, as some are in the habit of doing, but encouraging one another—and all the more as you see the Day approaching. (Hebrews 10 v 24-25)*

As with Deuteronomy in the old covenant, so with Hebrews in the new covenant: immersive discipleship through participation in the community of God's people is the key. And not simply once a week. There's a good chance that "the Day approaching" will fall off our radar if all we do is turn up on Sundays. The most compelling—the most "digital"—discipleship is drip-filtered.

So let's think about what that looks like.

Parental Discipleship

For all of the online influence that young people experience, survey after survey shows that the biggest influence on young people is still their parents.[27] As Christian parents, we are the most decisive factor—humanly speaking—in our children's lives. This means it's our responsibility to intentionally disciple our own children.

We need to lean away from outsourcing our parenting. Secular culture boasts that it can manage our children's upbringing from a younger and younger age in order to allow us to achieve maximum potential. And sure, paying for childcare or putting the kids in front of a screen for half an hour can provide a much-needed release of pressure on parents, as well as contributing to the kids' social development. But remember that the *Shema* calls on us to impress God's word upon our children when lying down and getting up, when at home and when walking along the road. Are we unquestioningly and repeatedly handing our children over to others—whether that's nursery workers or iPads—when they are at their most impressionable?

Christians need to start having the hard conversations now. We are heading into a more confronting post-Christian setting, in which online content and state intervention offer an increasingly ungodly discipleship program. What will we be willing to sacrifice to ensure that the discipleship of our children is of the godly kind? We need to ask ourselves how distracted we have allowed ourselves to become. If you're using technology as a baby-sitter while you get on with your own version of the good life, then don't be surprised at whose voices your children end up being shaped by.

It's not enough simply to try to police their viewing habits—though of course that will help. Don't underestimate the godly influence you can have simply through a steady diet of deliberately having meals together, praying in the car on the way to school, or using spare time to hang out. Counter-discipleship is drip-filtered first and foremost by parents.

My wife and I sometimes pack our two children (one a teenager, the other in her early twenties) into the car on a listless evening and drive into the city, buying a hot chocolate on the go. We take turns to choose songs on Spotify, explaining why we like them. It's a fun way to chat about the deeper things of life. Turns out, you'll learn a lot from Tyler the Creator's lyrics—for good or ill!

Community Discipleship

As Christian communities, how are we take the *Shema* command seriously in a corporate sense?

One way is to lean towards helping others, and lean away from the individualism and atomisation of our culture. Perhaps we could help the single parents who have to work full time and are struggling to spend time with their children, and for whom outsourcing parenting to an iPad is a fairly attractive option. I mentioned this in the previous chapter, but I'll say it again: what would it look like to intentionally include single parents and their children in our traditionally nuclear-family activities?

Another way is to think about the attitudes we display in our churches to key "discipleship issues" like money and sex. Do we proclaim a culture of contentment and generosity—and put that into practice? Do we hold out something genuinely better to those who are tempted by sexual immorality? Do we provide a depth and richness of communal life that puts online alternatives in the shade?

Perhaps the most obvious area to think about is how we help our young people to become part of our church communities. My daughter now works for the church that I planted. The key to her discipleship in her teens was the availability of several girls around five to seven years older than her who discipled her—taking her out for coffee and Bible, or just hanging out and inviting her to their events. She was immersed in a group of women whom she wanted to emulate. By the time she got to university, she already had a "digital" level of discipleship. In fact, she often remarked on the lack of community life and deep friendship on campus.

Of course, the content is also as important as the context. Digital discipleship must offer a *biblical* vision of human flourishing. We can no longer get away with an "evangelical-lite" youth program that is just games and a tacked-on short talk that avoids anything deep, or a hyped-up sugar-rush mosh-pit worship experience. Young people are looking for something solid and rich to base their lives upon—and a theology-rich, historically informed, 360-degree Christianity is what they need.

Detox Evangelism

Deep, rich community really works. Pastor and author Daniel Sih describes the impact of community meals without screens in his setting:

> During community meals we don't use phones, because we decided early on to avoid screens at our table. It wasn't a strict rule, but a community norm. When others began to join us, they unconsciously imitated our practices, and a culture formed ... By starting a consistent pattern, we have unwittingly created a community of people who share a digital parenting philosophy. Not everyone has the same rules, but we do support each other.[28]

Sih talks about the "aunties and uncles" in this community who share in the task of helping disciple each other's children. In time the meals even became an evangelistic opportunity as non-Christian parents shared their worries about the same issues with technology and screens. They were first intrigued and then excited by strategies to escape the all-encompassing online life. What they found themselves being invited into was not just an hour without screens but a community of grace, wisdom, truth and hope.

I want to close by saying that technology is not in itself the enemy. It just brings us new ways to be drawn in by the same old enticements—selfishness, sexual immorality, lust for wealth and so on. Which is why all we need, really, is the age-old deep discipleship we're called to by the likes of Deuteronomy and Hebrews.

But by the same token, technology can also provide new ways to be drawn in by the beauty of the gospel. If the online world *is* the real world for younger generations, then what world are we creating? Christians can paint a picture of God and his kingdom online—so let's make it a picture that is beautiful, rich and true, not reactionary, angry and divisive.

We need content creators who have deep, creatively compelling and biblically rich stories to tell—on whatever platform is available to them. A wry, think-about-it TikTok can be just as significant as a longform blog essay. It's time to work together as Christian creatives to come up with ever more compelling ways to use digital platforms to do "digital" discipleship.

I don't know what technological revelations are around the corner. Many good things will come, for sure. But as with all sinful human ventures, they will undoubtedly be more immersive, more compelling, often more toxic and definitely with more capacity to manipulate and divide us. They will pitch us a compelling vision of life. Only a more compelling "digital" discipleship program will counter it. And we have one.

7. The Culture Wars: How to Flourish as a Citizen

Kate Forbes would have made a great political leader. As a young woman and a parliamentary member for the Scottish National Party, Forbes has been a shining light in a Scottish government seeking independence from the United Kingdom. She was Scotland's Secretary for Finance and the Economy from the tender age of 29 in 2020 up until 2023, when she returned to the backbenches of the Scottish Parliament.

What is a talent like Kate Forbes doing on the backbenches, when young, skilled and articulate women are at a premium in politics? Well, here's the rub. Kate Forbes is an evangelical Christian, and her great crime is, well, to be an evangelical Christian. One with orthodox Christian views.

Long before she was in Parliament, Scotland voted for same-sex marriage. Forbes is on record as saying that she would have voted against it. So when Scotland's First Minister, Nicola Sturgeon, resigned, things heated up. Suddenly thrust into the spotlight as the naturally gifted frontrunner in the party leadership election, Forbes' views on sexuality, reproduction and gender were ruled contentious. How could she lead a political party in a modern, liberal Scotland? *The Guardian* newspaper put it like this:

> *Though in principle Forbes might appear a natural successor, she has made no secret about the strength of her religious beliefs ... It was revealed that in 2018, while still a backbencher but already tipped as a "rising star", she told an audience at a prayer breakfast that politicians should recognise that the treatment of the "unborn" was a "measure of true progress".*[29]

The conclusion was clear: Forbes' faith, the foundation of her stated desire to see justice and social change in Scotland, was an impediment to public leadership. In the end, the SNP voted in someone else—someone whose record across three departments in his time in Parliament had been less than impressive.

This issue is not just political, as the media interest shows. Increasingly, only one view of the complex matters around human identity is viewed as valid. Religious perspectives, Christian or not, that do not align with "the right side of history" in the culture wars are picked apart as reactionary or even unsafe.

Christians will often find themselves on the same side as the progressive culture warriors. Kate Forbes does on issues like tolerance, equality, justice and diversity. But when it comes to human identity issues? There's a huge gulf between a biblical view of human identity and purpose and the secular understanding.

Now this is just one example, but it shows where we've gotten to. We have a culture war on our hands. A war not only about gender and sexuality but also about freedom of speech, immigration, abortion and more. A war in which each viewpoint is held with deep conviction and ferocity, and in which the other side is labelled evil and dangerous. And a war that is particularly confronting to Christians.

It's Coming for You

There's a saying: "You may not be interested in war, but war is interested in you". If your country is under threat, ignoring or denying it won't stop your town being invaded and your house destroyed. Or your only son being drafted. The same is true of the culture wars. The church may have wished to stay away from the front line, but the front line has moved quickly to the church's doors. And there's no escaping the bombardment. The culture war is interested in us.

To take a few examples: let's say your children come home from school saying they've been shown a video of two men kissing and asked to say what they think about it. Do you call the school or do you ignore it and avoid trouble? Or a workmate demands that you use an unexpected set of pronouns. Do you do as you're asked, try to explain why you won't, or just avoid that person? Your faith-based school finds itself on the front page for not celebrating Pride Month, and it falls to you to write a press release rejecting the allegation that your school is unsafe. Interested now?

Secular culture increasingly demands that we fall into line. There's a new model citizen out there: one who prioritises individual expression, independence and self-actualisation above all else. That's who we're all supposed to be.

But Christian beliefs in God's purposes and plan for human flourishing are not compatible with this. So, the question becomes, "Can Christians take part in civic life in positive ways that allow us to maintain our distinctives?"

It's tempting to say no—we've got to raise the white flag for the sake of a quiet life. We quietly affirm chosen gender identities—after all, what positive difference can it possibly make if we refuse? Others do the opposite, saying that we should align ourselves with reactionary political forces. They may be distasteful, but at least they line up with conservative views on abortion or distinct roles for men and women in marriage.

The arguments go back and forth between Christians all the time. And I'd be the first to acknowledge that these issues are complex. Yet despite the complexities, I firmly believe that we *can* take part positively in civic life, while holding to what we know to be true. In a culture riven by anxiety and clashing viewpoints, we have something very important to offer.

Christians as Dual Citizens

The tension in the Bible is that God's people belong to two places: two worlds, two countries, two cities. Our earthly lives are lived "here", but we have another home "there". Like God's people in the Old Testament, we are "longing for a better country—a heavenly one" (Hebrews 11 v 16).

You might think that that means we should thumb our nose at earthly authorities. And we do see that happen often: Christians declare on social media or through civil disobedience that they do not recognise the government's values, or they call for the nation to return to its Christian roots. For some at the more extreme end, it becomes about withholding taxes or going off-grid. Most of us just have a growing sense of unease that we should be "doing more" to change how the government acts.

But it's more complex than that. Have a look at what Paul says to the Christians in Rome about their attitude to their rulers:

> *Let everyone be subject to the governing*
> *authorities, for there is no authority except that*
> *which God has established. The authorities that*

exist have been established by God. Consequently, whoever rebels against the authority is rebelling against what God has instituted, and those who do so will bring judgment on themselves. For rulers hold no terror for those who do right, but for those who do wrong. Do you want to be free from fear of the one in authority? Then do what is right and you will be commended. For the one in authority is God's servant for your good. But if you do wrong, be afraid, for rulers do not bear the sword for no reason. They are God's servants, agents of wrath to bring punishment on the wrongdoer. Therefore, it is necessary to submit to the authorities, not only because of possible punishment but also as a matter of conscience. (Romans 13 v 1-5)

In a pre-modern, non-democratic setting, Paul was being a realist. Obeying the laws of the land makes sense, especially if they're established by rulers outside our power. But Paul was not simply being pragmatic. He was also being theological. We should obey the law because God has established the authorities. They are ultimately under his authority. Obedience to the temporal powers reflects obedience to a God of order (1 Corinthians 14 v 33).

Now this is not the New Testament's final word on temporal power. There are situations in which disobedience—whether to civil laws or to societal expectations—is not only admissible but required if one is to be faithful to the Lord Jesus. We see this in 1 Peter: "If you suffer as a Christian, do not be ashamed" (4 v 16).

Peter acknowledges that godly behaviour will sometimes incur punishment. At his stage of history, persecution was localised and sporadic, but it would later become part of legislation as Christians refused to acknowledge Caesar as lord.

In normal circumstances, however, we are to obey the law of the land and submit to the authorities. Far from turning our backs completely on the world's ways of doing things, we are to seek to be good citizens of earth. And this is part of being a godly citizen of heaven.

In Romans 13 Paul is removing the blinders on the Roman Christians' eyes. Faced as they were with pagan earthly splendour that was clothed in tyranny and with a mantra of "Caesar is lord", it was possible to conclude that the situation was hopeless: the only alternatives were to reject and rebel against the wicked pagan authorities or to quake in fear of them and seek to avoid any kind of conflict.

But not to Paul. *Put on your transcendence glasses*, he urges them. *Let the fog clear, and see reality.* Rome only ruled because God permitted it. So these Christians didn't need to be angry or afraid. And nor do we.

Wisdom and Politics

Secular politics is not the be-all and end-all of our Christian hope. This should mean that Christians become curiosities in a deeply divided world. Christians will lean towards what are traditionally viewed as more progressive ideas on some matters and towards more conservative views on others, as they pursue what is right rather than what their party demands. For example, many evangelical churches I know have a keen interest in helping refugees, and seek to engage with social services such as foster care. Yet Christians will also lean towards more supposedly conservative ideas, with a commitment to right to life from womb to tomb. The Christian citizen should be a discombobulating experience to partisan politics, as we sound less black-and-white than secular voices—and not so blue or red.

Hence Christians can belong to both sides of the political fence—and make a difference to them both. If Daniel could be a chief adviser to the Babylonian king, then Christians can inhabit the geo-political world, bringing wisdom and temperance to it.

This doesn't only apply to the government kind of politics. Daniel wasn't just a political leader; he was a worker, dealing with colleagues and sitting at a desk. I'd like to think he applied the same wisdom to palace politics as he did to national concerns. We've all heard of office politics. Teachers are familiar with staffroom politics. In our workplaces, what if we were known as those who, when gossip came to us, killed it off so that it went no further? What if those who are hostile to the gospel knew that we could be counted on to say yes and mean it? What if the other mums at the school gate knew that you would not go along with the almost casual bullying and isolating of the newcomer who doesn't fit the mould or whose children are "problematic"?

I mentioned earlier the "new model citizen" that our culture wants us to be. But notice that this new model citizen has some design features we Christians would recognise. The ideal citizen for our world is a fully autonomous person who does what they want—but they are also a generous neighbour. This citizen does "You do you" and practices "Love is love"—yet they are also selfless and never damage anyone else. This citizen constantly upholds the dignity of the weakest, sickest and smallest—even while they enthusiastically embrace the idea that humanity is not created in the image of God.

The new model citizen, in other words, is self-actualised but also selfless. That's a contradiction, and it cannot hold. But it shows us where there is a place for Christians to contribute in positive ways to civic life. We might not be pursuing self-actualisation, but we can certainly pursue selflessness—and, with God's help, we can do it better than anyone else.

When Two Worlds Collide

Even so, sometimes it's more complicated than that. What happens when the two worlds collide? There are some situations where our culture's self-actualisation morality runs directly counter to what the Lord commands. In situations like those, how can we be good citizens in the eyes of the government, the media, and our neighbours, while being a godly citizen in the eyes of the Lord? Paul shows that it is complex but possible:

> *Do not repay anyone evil for evil. Be careful to do what is right in the eyes of everyone. If it is possible, as far as it depends on you, live at peace with everyone. Do not take revenge, my dear friends, but leave room for God's wrath, for it is written: "It is mine to avenge; I will repay," says the Lord. On the contrary:*
>
> *"If your enemy is hungry, feed him;*
> *if he is thirsty, give him something to drink.*
> *In doing this, you will heap burning coals*
> *on his head."*
>
> *Do not be overcome by evil, but overcome evil with good. (Romans 12 v 17-21)*

Paul is not so pious as to assume that Christians won't have enemies. Yet our response is not to be vengeance. It is to leave room for God. Specifically, to leave room for *his* vengeance!

The secular assumption in recent decades was that once we left the idea of a vengeful God behind us, society would become more tolerant and forgiving. This has been shown up as fanciful. With God out of the picture, we've outsourced vengeance—to ourselves. Witness the swarm mentality on Twitter, the cancel culture, the public shaming of those who fall foul of the accepted moral frameworks.

Faced with such hostility, most people put their heads down and avoid engagement with their enemies. Yet dissociation is not Paul's way. He tells us to overcome evil by doing good, not by doing nothing. While the world may not see our opinions as good, they won't be able to deny the goodness of our actions if we live as God commands.

Seeking the good of a cultural enemy is the cross-shaped way to live as citizens of heaven. This could be reaching out privately to someone with whom you've had a dispute, to see if you can resolve the matter and come to some agreement. Or simply refusing to hold a grudge. Or putting your own interests aside and celebrating and encouraging the one whose project got the nod instead of yours.

A progressive work colleague charged with rolling out a celebration-of-identity program may need to hear that as a Christian you want all colleagues to be given dignity and affirmed as valuable. Having a conversation about how that can also include religious minorities (including those who are perhaps even more conservative around sexuality issues than you are) can be a place to find common ground—and common good.

Yet Paul is realistic. He includes the phrases "if it is possible" and "as far as it depends on you". Sometimes, no matter how peaceable we want to be, it won't be possible! So, Christians may assure the LGBTQI+ community that although they don't wish to celebrate certain lifestyles, the gospel gives us the power and desire to love people— but they repeatedly find that this is viewed by the wider culture as a mask for bigotry and hatred. Even so, it is still possible for us to be patient and peaceable as we face vitriol and opposition—and as we pursue peace while sticking to biblical truth, we can be confident that we are being godly citizens of heaven.

Living at Peace in Wartime

I would need a whole separate book to cover every issue in the culture wars in sufficient detail! A lot of the working out of how to overcome evil with good in the modern age will have to be done by individuals and churches on a case-by-case basis. But, to get you started, here is a highlights tour.

There are tensions over issues of free speech versus trigger warnings. Do we have the right to say what we wish to say in a democracy? Much of the time we do—though even that is changing. But in order to be careful to do what is right in the eyes of everyone, we need to think through *how* we use our freedom to speak. The Bible does not talk about free speech, but it does talk about wise speech, which means being "slow to speak" and "quick to listen" (James 1 v 19-20). That command alone would kill off a lot of our social-media interactions.

Then there's race and diversity. Should our first response to "Black Lives Matter" merely be "All lives matter"? Do we have to jump straight into a defence of the created equality of all humans from the get-go, particularly when there are real racial grievances? The church has the opportunity to model true diversity by bringing people together and genuinely listening to—and equipping for leadership—minority groups within our midst. On this issue and others, Christians can model a way that offers forgiveness, accepts limitations, and refuses to crush opponents. A way that can bring about the unity that so many progressive narratives desire but struggle to attain.

And what about abortion? It's easy for Christians to mainline on YouTube videos of whip-smart conservatives slapping down college students over this issue. (Oh, you haven't seen that online cottage industry yet?) It's harder—and more costly—to consider how to help fund and support new and pregnant mothers, not simply reactively but proactively. For those considering abortions, and indeed those who have had them, the church can become known as a place that will offer help in time of need—and grace in time of failure.

There's the question of pronoun usage. Is this always black-and-white? A Christian psychotherapist may wish to invoke their right not to use the preferred pronouns of a trans client, yet in the clinical setting it may be more loving—and helpful to the process—to do so. In the absence of clear commands, the gospel gives us liberty to align with our conscience, and there are plenty of reasons both for and against using the pronouns a person prefers. Above all, we should remember that not every trans person we meet is a woke activist. Most just wish to get on with their lives quietly—and many have a history of trauma and pain that requires our compassion, even if we profoundly disagree with their life choices.

Overcoming evil with good might not result in us getting "our way" in the culture wars. It might not mean that our political, educational or ecclesiastical efforts will win the day. Evil will ultimately be overcome by good only when Jesus returns. Our culture will continue to call good evil and evil good despite our best efforts to model true goodness. But as dual citizens of heaven and earth, we can afford to wait.

Educating for Wartime

The current culture war is still primarily a "cold war". Yet the signs indicate that the next generation of God's people will likely experience a "hot war" that seeks to completely suffocate any compelling public Christian witness. It will conscript the corporate, legal, academic and educational spheres to ensure victory.

One area that seems to be particularly in the crosshairs of progressive governments is schooling. The moral formation of the secular education system is designed to produce model citizens who will help us move towards a more just and equitable society. So far, so good. That's what a Christian education system desires also. Yet their methods are odds with each other. Christianity's doctrine of human flourishing is now regarded as part of society's problem, not part of its solution.

There's no single "right way" to educate our children. Some will decide to homeschool or send children to a Christian school, in order to avoid the indoctrination of secular public schools. If you do choose public schooling—or it's your only option—it's worth remembering that parents must remain invested in their children's education. Perhaps you won't be able to influence the curriculum, but it's important to keep asking questions—of your children and of the system. Remind children of how God calls us to live faithfully in the world and not simply withdraw from it. Yet at the same time help them to keep a critical mindset towards the views they are hearing.

I'm encouraged to think of my French friend who, growing up, was the only Christian in a high school of 4,000 students. In a deeply secular country, he knew what it was to be in a minority! Yet his small evangelical church experience was deep and rich. And far more compelling than school.

Christianity is most compelling when its message is embedded within communities that clearly show how liveable its truths are—how emotionally, relationally and intellectually compelling they are. It's counterintuitive, but in tough times for the church—with shrinking attendance and scandals being played out before a gleeful media—our tactic should be to raise the bar, not lower it, by creating Christian communities that live for Jesus by standing up for what is good. We are educating for wartime, and the time to start that is now.

I know of the CEO of a Christian schools association, who is working with government officials to reframe the online schools rankings. Schools had been discouraging lower-achieving students from accessing tertiary-entrance subjects, partly because of the risk of receiving a lower ranking. It's not a good look! The CEO told the government that as an association of Christian schools, he and his colleagues were determined to lead the way in giving every student access to the subjects they wished to do, for *their* sake, and not merely to make the school look good. This is not the kind of action that hits the headlines necessarily, but it makes a difference. And it is a small way of showing why the gospel is plausible. Not only plausible, actually, but vital.

Here's the encouragement: there is a King above who still rules and reigns, despite the secular culture's insistence otherwise. The culture war is, in the end, a phoney war; the true battle has been fought and won by King Jesus over the powers and principalities. What we are experiencing are the retreating skirmishes of a vanquished foe—rebellious citizens who have usurped their true King in the vain hope of claiming territory they do not own. But we have true hope:

> But our citizenship is in heaven. And we eagerly
> await a Savior from there, the Lord Jesus Christ,
> who, by the power that enables him to bring
> everything under his control, will transform our
> lowly bodies so that they will be like his glorious
> body. (Philippians 3 v 20-21)

8. Ecology: How to Flourish as a Steward

Louise Harris was sobbing atop a gantry on London's major ring road, the M25. The 24-year-old Cambridge University student was filming herself as part of a protest for the Just Stop Oil organisation that brought traffic to a standstill for more than five hours on one of the UK's busiest motorways. Louise wailed into the camera in a moment that went viral online, declaring, "You might hate me for doing this. I'm here because I don't have a future."

Louise is not alone. Many younger people have come to the same conclusion. They have no future because of the changing climate. What's the point of anything at all if the planet is going to burn up because of human folly? The level of anxiety over the idea of a climate crisis has created a crisis climate.

Nothing divides like views on climate change. It's a real "best of times / worst of times" moment. Louise's efforts were lauded in one newspaper, while another posted photographs of her in her petrol-driven car, insinuating that her display of anguish was hypocritical. There is climate-change crisis and climate-change denial. The science is either settled or the science is politically driven for the sake of grant money. There are generational and political differences on what can be done. There are countries calling for other countries to change, while conveniently neglecting their own responsibilities. Everyone's got an opinion on the climate.

The result is, as you'd expect, confusion. But not only confusion. Also despair, guilt, a sense of foreboding and shame—a shame that sees many of us trying to do our little bit by sorting our recycling carefully, but secretly wondering whether there's any point. There's anger at what's happened to the planet and at the stress of poorer, low-lying countries who face rising sea levels. There is worry at the rising levels of consumption and a vague sense of guilt. But the guilt doesn't seem to be enough to stop us buying, flying, holidaying, upgrading, refurbishing. It's as if it's so overwhelming that we just block it out. Until someone like Louise Harris turns up the volume.

Christians aren't immune from the confusion around climate issues, nor from the oscillation between guilt and denial. That means there are just as many responses and just as many divisions among God's people about the source and depth of and the solution to the problem—or even if there is a problem at all.

This chapter is designed to help us pick our way through the detritus. Not by nailing all of the issues—I am no expert on biodiversity, recycling or the pros and cons of electric cars—but by pitching a vision for the future that's grounded in Scripture. Unlike Louise, God's people know that we *do* have a future, and a hope-filled one at that. The biblical understanding of creation—where it has come from, why it's like it is, and what direction it is heading in—will enable us to be wise stewards who honour what God has given us, but also joyful stewards who hope for what God has promised us. While we might not all be perfectly clued up on everything that needs to be done, we do have a better, more hope-filled perspective to offer to those who are also struggling to make sense of it all.

A Good but Groaning Planet

When it comes to the state of the planet, Christians should be the most realistic of all people about the state of play. The Genesis account of creation (Genesis 1 – 2) tells us that God created everything "good" or "very good" (e.g. 1 v 4, 25). The term "good" means that before sin entered the world, the direction of the created order was unimpeded because the fall had not yet happened. Each part of the creation fulfilled its function in the way God intended.

Sin disrupted this. We can't read Genesis 1 – 2 without Genesis 3 if we are to have a robust understanding of what is happening in God's good creation. Human rebellion has marred every aspect of the created order, starting with the pinnacle of God's creation—humans themselves—but trickling all the way down the food chain. When you prick your finger on a thorn while gardening, it is more than just an annoyance. It is a reminder that sin stains everything in creation.

We cannot underestimate the pervasive impact of sin, not only on our will (what we wish to do) but on our wisdom (what we think is the right thing to do) as well. When it comes to our will, one consequence of the fall is that we are rebellious. We are, as Augustine stated, and Luther restated, "curved in on ourselves"[30]—that's what sin does to us. We justify many of the decisions we make simply on the basis that we want to make them. This is true of our care of the planet also. We refuse to see that vast amounts of clothing are wasted because of our commitment to fashion. We're willing to turn a blind eye to the waste we contribute to the world's rubbish heaps if it suits us. That's one example of how sin affected our will.

And our wisdom? Another result of the fall is that we are *unwise*. We are blind to solutions that we should have seen, and we plunge into problems that we thought would be solutions. Unintended consequences are everywhere. When it comes to the climate, we're playing a planetary game of Whack-a-Mole, pushing down one problem while another one pops up. For example, electric vehicles are mooted as the answer to fossil-fuel consumption. But the manner in which the minerals for battery production are sourced is often unethical, damaging some of the planet's poorest people.[31]

Other good intentions get scuppered by other people—as observed by a friend of mine involved in a global NGO that helps supply fresh water. You would think that providing fresh running water to a slum in India would help those living there. But guess what? Those slums are owned by landlords. The minute fresh water goes in, the attractiveness of the area goes up. The slum-dwellers face a rent hike they cannot pay and are forced to move out, while other people who can pay the higher rent move in. It's Whack-a-Mole again.

Secular perspectives on climate change tend towards blaming others for the problem. It's big oil, or it's big pharma, or it's big whatever. But the problem of sin starts off little—and it's lodged in every human heart. Christians can be the most realistic about how bad things are because we, above all others, ought to be realistic about ourselves as central to the problem. There's no room for self-justification among Christians in this realm, nor should there be a sense that other people are the problem and not us. We're all the problem because "all have sinned" (Romans 3 v 23). Maybe big oil companies or particular governments are the ones responsible for that emission or this waste dump, but the Bible is clear that there's one overarching reason why the world is groaning—and it's the sin of every one of us. The whole world is in "bondage to decay" as a direct result of the fall (Romans 3 v 20-23).

That all sounds like a litany of disaster. Yet, rather than self-loathing, despair or denial, the Bible gives us a profound hope for where the planet is heading. While the current environment is a good—though marred—gift from God, it is not our ultimate hope.

A New Earth

World Environment Day 2022 ran with the slogan "Only One Earth". There's truth to that. Yet the Bible builds a surprising and delightfully hope-filled narrative of *new creation*—a narrative that promises continuity with the current created order while also building discontinuity into the story. Is there only one earth that we should take care of? Yes. Will the earth be renewed by God regardless of our human interventions? Yes. Turns out the story of creation renewal is both/and.

What is the exact relationship between the continuity and the discontinuity? It's hard to say. Romans 8 points to continuity through deep renewal: "The creation itself will be liberated from its bondage to decay" (v 21). On the other hand, the letter of 2 Peter suggests deep deconstruction:

> But the day of the Lord will come like a thief.
> The heavens will disappear with a roar; the
> elements will be destroyed by fire, and the earth
> and everything done in it will be laid bare. Since
> everything will be destroyed in this way, what
> kind of people ought you to be? You ought to live

holy and godly lives as you look forward to the day
of God and speed its coming. That day will bring
about the destruction of the heavens by fire, and the
elements will melt in the heat. But in keeping with
his promise we are looking forward to a new heaven
and a new earth, where righteousness dwells.

(2 Peter 3 v 10-13)

And then there are these words in Revelation, which refer
to a prophecy first made to Israel in Isaiah 65 v 17:

Then I saw "a new heaven and a new earth", for the
first heaven and the first earth had passed away,
and there was no longer any sea.

(Revelation 21 v 1)

These passages about destruction and newness should
not lull us into thinking we can do what we like with the
planet. The true key to continuity and discontinuity is
found, as ever, in the person of Jesus. The resurrected
Jesus is continuous with who he was prior to his death, but
also discontinuous, in the sense that he is now glorified
and can never suffer death again. It will be the same with
our own bodies. Why does the 2 Peter passage above not
just say that we can do what we like with our bodies, since
everything will be burned up? Because our resurrection,
like Christ's, will have continuity and discontinuity to it.
We will plainly be "us", but we will also have new bodies.

We can take that same "both/and" attitude to how the rest
of creation will be viewed by God in the resurrection age.

We don't know exactly what will be renewed and what will be destroyed. But the promise of a new creation calls us to steward the current creation carefully. Just as we should not sin sexually, for example, because in the resurrection we will be judged for "things done while in the body" (2 Corinthians 5 v 10), so we should assume that deeds done to the planet by those same bodies have meaning and significance in the new age too—because the new planet will have a "memory" of the old one.

Human-Filled, Not Human-less

So the Bible story doesn't just leave us in the woeful mire of pointing out the problem. It offers a solution. And as we think about what to do now as we look forward to that perfect future, we should be clear that the Bible sees us—humans—as a fundamental part of it. But we are promised a renewed creation only in the context of a renewed humanity. Romans 8 puts it like this:

> For the creation waits in eager expectation for the children of God to be revealed. For the creation was subjected to frustration, not by its own choice, but by the will of the one who subjected it, in hope that the creation itself will be liberated from its bondage to decay and brought into the freedom and glory of the children of God. (v 19-21)

The creation isn't longing for us to shuffle off into gory death or be uploaded into a machine. It's waiting for us—

the children of God, all those who trust in Christ—to be shifted into glorious life! It will be completed and restored only when we are. The future is a hopeful, human-filled renewed creation—a resurrection future of glorious humanity, the children of God, who will have the wisdom and purity to sustainably work the new creation to God's purposes and for his glory.

In the 2018 Marvel movie *Avengers: Infinity War,* there's a moment when the interstellar warlord Thanos sits down peacefully to enjoy the sunset. Delightful. Except he has just been responsible for the destruction of half the sentient beings in the universe, including 50% of Earth's population, using a random process called the Blip.

The gentle pastoral music accompanying the bucolic scene is beguiling. Thanos smiles contentedly as he surveys the unsullied beauty before him. Why is he so happy? Because maybe the universe has a future after all. Thanos' reasoning is clear, even if his methods are appalling:

> *It's a simple calculus. This universe is finite, its resources finite. If life is left unchecked, life will cease to exist.*

Sound far-fetched? It is the Marvel universe, after all. Yet over recent decades, the idea that we could save the planet if the number of humans were vastly reduced has taken hold. Back in 2006, the ecologist Eric Pianka told a Texas Academy of Science meeting that 90% of humans had to die to save the planet. Pianka enthusiastically endorsed a widespread disease to control what he called "the scourge of humanity". He ended with this flourish: "We're looking forward to a huge collapse".[32] Some people make Thanos look conservative!

Of course, for most of us, the gut reflex is to celebrate not the destruction of humanity but the protection of it. The COVID lockdowns were a case in point. Pianka might have seen the pandemic as a golden opportunity to let a disease savage the global population—but of course that's not what happened. Whole countries closed their borders, some for years on end, because something in us values our collective humanity. We don't sneer as we watch humans suffer and merely think, "There goes a fat human biomass".

Even so, we struggle to envisage humanity and creation flourishing side by side. Regardless of where we pin the blame for today's planetary problems, the issues can seem impossible to reconcile. Can we really find a way of cutting consumption without plunging more people into poverty? Can we really give nature a chance without compromising food production? Can human flourishing and creation flourishing really coexist?

Complete success in this may be beyond us. But as Romans 8 shows, it is not beyond God.

All of this tells us something important about what the creation is *for*. As Christians we have a vision of the planet's future that goes beyond continuity for continuity's sake. The Westminster Shorter Catechism puts it like this:

Q: What is the chief end of man?
A: Man's chief end is to glorify God and enjoy him
for ever.

So whether you eat or drink or whatever you do, do
all to the glory of God. (1 Corinthians 10 v 31)

Christians are convinced by the hope of the resurrection that our goal is to enjoy God in a perfected creation, the goodness of which will no longer be derailed by our sin. To enjoy God for ever will not mean existing as a disembodied piece of gossamer floating in the ether playing a harp. The groaning of the planet will lead to the rebirthing of the planet—with humans front and centre.

Both the created world and the humans that live in it have dignity and purpose. As we look to our future, we must not let concerns about the environment cause us to lose sight of God's love for people. Nor should we let concerns about people cause us to forget the goodness of the world that will one day be renewed to share our freedom as God's children. Once again, it's both/and.

A Glimpse of the Future

The good news is that, in God's grace, we don't have to wait until the last day for both the creation and humans to be dignified. One of the most inspiring ecological stories I have heard is that of Christian agronomist Tony Rinaudo, whose book *The Forest Underground: Hope for a Planet in Crisis* was 2022 Australian Christian Book of the Year.

Together with his wife, Liz, Tony spent years working in the degraded farming landscape of Niger. His expertise led to a revitalisation of entire communities whose farming practices had been blind to a simple reality: reviving damaged trees whose roots were still extant was more effective than planting new trees.

Sounds simple. But it has been life-changing. Tony's technique, now called Farmer-Managed Natural Regeneration, has regreened more than 18 million hectares in 27 countries, reduced carbon footprints and fed millions of people, saving lives and livelihoods. Tony has received major national and international awards for his work. Crucially, Tony loves humans *and* the planet because he loves the God who created both.

We can't all be Tony Rinaudos—although one reader might well be the next Tony—but we can all love both humans and the planet in ways that matter around us. We can't do everything, but we can do something. And however miniscule our actions may seem, they can also contribute to our goal to ensure that those who don't yet have a gospel hope can see the difference Jesus makes in the nooks and crannies of our lives.

Materialist But Not Materialistic

When it comes to being human, matter matters. Christians are materialists in the best sense of that word, not least of all because we believe in the resurrection of the body! This means we take material things seriously. How we treat "other stuff" is as theologically driven, and as important, as how we treat other humans.

And so we ought not to be *materialistic*. By that I mean we shouldn't be driven only by material concerns in such a way that everything becomes a commodity for our satisfaction. Jesus himself points out the futility of that pursuit when he says:

> *So do not worry, saying, "What shall we eat?" or*
> *"What shall we drink?" or "What shall we wear?"*
> *For the pagans run after all these things, and your*
> *heavenly Father knows that you need them. But*
> *seek first his kingdom and his righteousness, and all*
> *these things will be given to you as well.*
>
> *(Matthew 6 v 31-33)*

The great tragedy of our Western society is that we have never had so much stuff and have never been less content! We *want* to give up wanting when we see how our excesses affect our environment, but we struggle to stop wanting and often justify ourselves when we give in to our wants. But this is where Christians can lead the way. Our default should be contentment, not running after things.

The idea of contentment runs through the Old and New Testaments. When God laid down Sabbath laws for Israel, he was saying, *I am your true Sustainer*. Every other nation could stay busy buying and selling and working seven days per week, but Yahweh would sustain his people in and by their rest.

And when we turn to the New Testament, contentment is ramped up as we read:

> *Keep your lives free from the love of money and be content with what you have, because God has said, "Never will I leave you; never will I forsake you."*
> *(Hebrews 13 v 5)*

And:

> *Command those who are rich in this present world not to be arrogant nor to put their hope in wealth, which is so uncertain, but to put their hope in God, who richly provides us with everything for our enjoyment. (1 Timothy 6 v 17)*

What might it look like for Christians to live plainly and simply in a world that always seeks the next thing? And to do so in a way that raises questions from unbelievers about the source of our contentment? Perhaps it's as simple as encouraging each other to be content with what we have and committing ourselves to finding our contentment in the riches of the grace of the gospel.

Having people with whom we can be transparent about our spending habits is important. You don't need to hand over authority to anyone else in making such decisions, but given that wealth is the blind spot of the modern West, don't assume you are immune from greed! There should be a commitment by the church to teach about money: how to use it well and how to ensure that over the course of our lives our default is to be generous in giving—all in light of the generosity of Jesus (2 Corinthians 8 v 7-9). We must also ask ourselves who we honour in the church. Are we the same as the evil judges of James 2, who preference the impressive and the wealthy? Or are we able to look at the heart?

And there are visible, practical steps we can take as a church community. The constant demand to upgrade technologies and styles of furnishing, both in church buildings and in our homes, should be treated carefully. How about conducting a "clothes register"—finding out who in your community can personally benefit from quality clothing (not just the cast-offs) that others don't need? Could your church create other registers for items that are often bought by individuals but used sporadically and whose use could be shared? Whatever the principle of contentment looks like for you, the point is to no longer live as if externals are the most important factor.

A Hope-Filled Apocalypse

One final observation. There's really no such thing as a "religion-less" approach to the environment. In fact, much of the secular climate movement has a religious feel and tone to it. In 2023, if you bump into someone on a street corner wearing a sandwich board around their neck with the words *"The End Is Nigh"* on it, they are far more likely to be a climate protester than a fundamentalist preacher.

Former Extinction Rebellion media employee Zion Lights claims that the climate movement has "a cult problem". Zion, who is still active in climate concerns, says that her experience with the organisation was overtly religious in tone. She describes the behaviour and adulation of one of Extinction Rebellion's co-founders, Roger Hallam, in terms that are eerily similar to those used by escapees from fundamentalist religious groups:

> *Roger knows his followers—mostly young men and women—feel immense guilt about their carbon-heavy lifestyles. He preys on their guilt and their anxiety about the future. You could almost describe Roger as the leader of a cult. For any cult to work it needs to offer salvation. Roger offers that, plus a sense of purpose and belonging to the young people who flock to him.*[33]

The message of climate activism is that apocalyptic, catastrophic climate events are coming. Hallam highlights the problem, but, as Zion observes, he can only tap into guilt, fear and anxiety to motivate his followers. Our gospel offers something better. We have a rescuer beyond ourselves; we have both grace and hope. Only grace can transform our hearts' desires—the very desires that have caused the selfish greed and myopic short-termism that have degraded our environment. And only a true and certain hope can rescue us from denial or despair.

A big vision of God's work of creation and new creation is the renewable energy source *par excellence*. The promised restoration of all creation *then* is the reason for our planetary care *now*. Let's ensure, no matter how this issue twists and turns, that over the coming decades we build a hope-filled—and human-filled—Christian ecology to offer the despairing Louises of this generation.

Afterword

I began writing this book during the queen's Platinum Jubilee celebrations. I wrote this afterword the day of the coronation of her son, King Charles III. A book about the future, bookended by one event looking to a tumultuous but now settled past and another event looking forward to a tumultuous and unsettled—and unsettling—future. Despite the self-conscious continuity of "The queen is dead; long live the king", so much has changed, and so much more is set to change.

There's sure to be plenty about the future that we will recognise, although many challenges will be more complex than we had imagined. But when it comes to the future, that's all that we have—our imaginations. There will be patterns that are familiar and problems we did not envisage. We will be blindsided both by trends that we could have predicted and by cataclysmic events that will only have seemed obvious on the other side of them. Welcome to history. That's how it has always been. And you can see how it makes people anxious! You can see how it tempts God's people to anxiety too.

What attitude should you take as you leave from reading this book and go forward? Perhaps the attitude of Daniel in exile in the Persian Empire. In the second half of the book of Daniel, its main character is given his own *Back to the Future* experience with a series of apocalyptic visions from God. He sees kings rise and fall and empires drag themselves out of the churn of history before eventually failing just like the rest. Above all, he sees a figure "like a son of man" rise and rule for ever: a truly human, truly divine King who holds the future in his hands (Daniel 7 v 13-14). This gives Daniel confidence.

Daniel isn't told everything about the future. Ultimately, he has to leave it in God's hands. But here's what he is told:

> *As for you, go your way till the end. You will rest,*
> *and then at the end of the days you will rise to*
> *receive your allotted inheritance. (Daniel 12 v 13)*

Daniel is futureproofed. Not by his insight. Not by his status or position. Not even by his Jewish pedigree. Daniel is futureproofed by the God who knows the future and who holds it in his hands.

The same is true for us. I think the suggestions and predictions in this book are reasonable—yet the future over the next decades may turn out very different. However, this much we know: one day, like Daniel, all of God's people will rise and receive their allotted inheritance in the eternal kingdom won for them by the

Son of Man—the Lord Jesus. Until that time, let's go our way, serving our King in joy and confidence, knowing that he has made us futureproof.

Acknowledgements

I'm grateful for the support from our Providence Church community in Perth, and the wider body of Christian leaders in our city who prayerfully consider how to navigate the future with gospel confidence and clarity. In particular, Mark, Binh and John: they are truly discerning the times.

In the wider Australian scene, many thanks to those who have been to workshops and events that I have spoken at, who have given me positive, fearless and instructive feedback. We need the wisdom of all of God's people.

Special shout out to Katy Morgan and her editing skills once again. A second book seemed more daunting than the first, but you made it work somehow!

Notes

1   Kim Hart, "Exclusive poll: Most Democrats see Republicans as racist, sexist", *Axios* (November 12, 2018): www.axios.com/2018/11/12/poll-democrats-and-republicans-hate-each-other-racist-ignorant-evil (accessed April 14, 2023).

2   Matthew Knott and Angus Thomson, "Abandoning God: Christianity plummets as 'non-religious' surges in census", *The Sydney Morning Herald* (June 28, 2022): www.smh.com.au/national/abandoning-god-christianity-plummets-as-non-religious-surges-in-census-20220627-p5awvz.html (accessed September 13, 2023).

3   Mark Sayers, *A Non-Anxious Presence* (Moody, 2022), p 41.

4   old.reddit.com/r/pics/comments/vlkine/pregnant_woman_protesting_against_supreme_court (accessed May 2, 2023).

5   Carl Trueman, *The Rise and Triumph of the Modern Self* (Crossway, 2020), p 63.

6   Wendy Tuohy, "'Our mental health is collectively breaking': One in five Australians had mental disorder in pandemic", *Sydney Morning Herald* (July 22, 2022): www.smh.com.au/national/one-in-five-australians-have-a-mental-health-disorder-abs-snapshot-finds-20220721-p5b3bz.html (accessed June 2, 2023).

7   Timothy Keller, "American Christianity Is Due for a Revival", *The Atlantic* (February 5, 2023): www.theatlantic.com/ideas/archive/2023/02/christianity-secularization-america-renewal-modernity/672948/ (accessed June 2, 2023).

8   Timothy Keller, *Forgive* (Hodder and Stoughton, 2022), p 31.

9   Michael Koziol, "'Not a single person will talk to you': Why it's so hard to make friends in Sydney", *The Sydney Morning Herald* (July 23, 2022): www.smh.com.au/national/nsw/not-a-single-person-will-talk-to-you-why-it-s-so-hard-to-make-friends-in-sydney-20220720-p5b37s.html (accessed July 23, 2022).

10 Elsa Silberstein, "FIFO miners' mental health in spotlight, amid calls for onsite psychologists", *ABC News* (August 8, 2021): www.abc.net.au/news/2021-08-08/fifo-mental-health-in-spotlight-calls-for-psychologists-at-mines/100357030 (accessed May 16, 2023).

11 Robert N. Bellah, "Unitarian Universalism in Societal Perspective", Unitarian Universalist Association General Assembly (June 27, 1998): hirr.hartsem.edu/bellah/lectures_7.htm (accessed June 1, 2023).

12 Tara Isabella Burton, "I Spent Years Searching for Magic—I Found God Instead", *Catapult* (October 1, 2019): catapult.co/stories/i-spent-years-searching-for-magici-found-god-instead-tara-isabella-burton (accessed June 2, 2023).

13 Grant Morrison, *Supergods* (Spiegel and Grau, 2011), p 4.

14 Joanna Howe, "The ACT's takeover of Calvary Hospital overrides conscientious objection and threatens religious freedom", *ABC News* (May 17, 2023): www.abc.net.au/religion/act-takeover-of-calvary-hospital-overrides-freedom-of-conscience/102356586 (accessed June 2, 2023).

15 See www.equalityaustralia.org.au/alrcreviewdelay (accessed June 2, 2023); Paul Karp, "Sydney Anglican church accuses law reform commission of double standard over religious school hiring", *The Guardian* (March 1, 2023): www.theguardian.com/australia-news/2023/mar/02/sydney-anglican-church-accuses-law-reform-commission-of-double-standard-over-religious-school-hiring (accessed June 2, 2023).

16 "'We don't trust in governments,' Scott Morrison tells Margaret Court's Perth Church", *The Guardian Australia* (July 19, 2022): www.youtube.com/watch?v=sCoCdCVBmT8&ab_channel=GuardianAustralia (accessed September 13, 2023).

17 Abraham Kuyper, "Sphere Sovereignty: A public address delivered at the inauguration of the Free University, Oct. 20, 1880", translated by George Kamps: media.thegospelcoalition.org/wp-content/uploads/2017/06/24130543/SphereSovereignty_English.pdf (accessed September 13, 2023).

18 Joseph Chamie, "Living alone in America", *The Hill* (July 19, 2021): www.thehill.com/opinion/finance/563786-living-alone-in-america/ (accessed April 25, 2023).

19 Sam Allberry, *What God Has to Say about Our Bodies* (Crossway, 2021), p 30.

20 Sam Allberry, *What God Has to Say about Our Bodies*, p 26.

21 Tara Isabella Burton, "The Problem With Letting Therapy-Speak Invade Everything", *The New York Times* (November 12, 2022): www.nytimes.com/2022/11/12/opinion/mental-health-therapy-instagram.html (accessed June 2, 2023).

22 David Brooks, "The Morality of Selfism", *The New York Times* (January 3, 2019): www.nytimes.com/2019/01/03/opinion/self-care-individualism.html (accessed May 2, 2023).

23 Josée Rose, "High-profile tech leaders say AI is developing too fast and we should pause. Google's Bard says it's complicated", *Insider* (April 1, 2023): www.businessinsider.com/ai-is-developing-too-fast-pause-bard-says-its-complicated-2023-4 (accessed May 6, 2023).

24 Jon Haidt, "Social Media Is a Major Cause of the Mental Illness Epidemic in Teen Girls. Here's the Evidence" (February 22, 2023): www.jonathanhaidt.substack.com/p/social-media-mental-illness-epidemic (accessed May 6, 2023).

25 Daniel Sih, *Raising Tech-Healthy Humans* (Publish Central, 2023), p 9.

26 Michael Flood, "Pornography has deeply troubling effects on young people, but there are ways we can minimise the harm", *The Conversation* (January 5, 2020): www.theconversation.com/pornography-has-deeply-troubling-effects-on-young-people-but-there-are-ways-we-can-minimise-the-harm-127319 (accessed May 6, 2023).

27 "Interview: Changing Parental Behavior with Behavioral Tools Can Help Children Reach their Full Potential", Inter-American Development Bank (August 6, 2018): blogs.iadb. org/desarrollo-infantil/en/parental-behavior-influences-child-development (accessed September 13, 2023).

28 Daniel Sih, *Space Maker* (100M Publishing, 2021), p 111-112.

29 Aubrey Allegretti, "Kate Forbes' religious beliefs could stall her bid to succeed Sturgeon", *The Guardian* (February 16, 2023): www.theguardian.com/politics/2023/feb/16/kate-forbes-sturgeon-successor-religious-beliefs (accessed April 25, 2023).

30 Quoted in Matt Jenson, *The Gravity of Sin* (T&T Clark, 2007), p 4.

31 "Human Rights in the Mineral Supply Chains of Electric Vehicles", *Business and Human Rights Resource Centre*: www.business-humanrights.org/en/from-us/briefings/transition-minerals-sector-case-studies/human-rights-in-the-mineral-supply-chains-of-electric-vehicles (accessed June 8, 2023).

32 Ronald Bailey, "To Save the Planet, Kill 90 Percent of People Off, Says UT Ecologist", *Reason* (March 4, 2006): www.reason.com/2006/04/03/to-save-the-planet-kill-90-per (accessed June 9, 2023).

33 Zion Lights, "Climate Activism Has a Cult Problem", *The Free Press* (January 23, 2023): www.thefp.com/p/climate-activism-has-a-cult-problem (accessed April 19, 2023).

For more from Stephen McAlpine...

Have you noticed that recently, Christian views aren't seen as merely false but dangerous—our opinions no longer worth considering but rather in need of silencing?

How did this happen?

How did Christians become the bad guys?

And what do we do about it now?

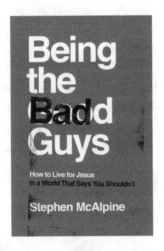

"Readers will come away with both a newfound boldness to live for Christ in a confusing world and a countercultural joy that will radiate in their public and private witness."
—Daniel Darling

COMPANY

BIBLICAL | RELEVANT | ACCESSIBLE

At The Good Book Company, we are dedicated to helping Christians and local churches grow. We believe that God's growth process always starts with hearing clearly what he has said to us through his timeless word—the Bible.

Ever since we opened our doors in 1991, we have been striving to produce Bible-based resources that bring glory to God. We have grown to become an international provider of user-friendly resources to the Christian community, with believers of all backgrounds and denominations using our books, Bible studies, devotionals, evangelistic resources, and DVD-based courses.

We want to equip ordinary Christians to live for Christ day by day, and churches to grow in their knowledge of God, their love for one another, and the effectiveness of their outreach.

Call us for a discussion of your needs or visit one of our local websites for more information on the resources and services we provide.

Your friends at The Good Book Company

thegoodbook.com | thegoodbook.co.uk
thegoodbook.com.au | thegoodbook.co.nz
thegoodbook.co.in